THE REFERENCE SHELF

Vol. 31 No. 3

REPRESENTATIVE AMERICAN SPEECHES: 1958-1959

Edited, and with Introductions
by
A. CRAIG BAIRD
Department of Speech, State University of Iowa

THE H. W. WILSON COMPANY
NEW YORK 1959

Printed in the United States of America
Library of Congress Catalog Card No. (38-27962)

PREFATORY NOTE

Representative American Speeches: 1958-1959 is the twenty-second in this annual series. Each volume contains some eighteen "representative" speeches by Americans or by others who have talked in this country (six of Winston Churchill's American speeches have been included). These volumes, beginning with the 1937-1938 compilation, contain more than four hundred addresses by more than three hundred orators. (The Cumulative Author Index contains the full list of speakers and their speeches.)

Classification of speeches. As in the previous volumes, the speeches have been grouped according to their subject matter, such as International Problems and Policies (summit talks, control of nuclear testing, national defense reorganization, foreign aid, reciprocal trade agreements, problems relating to Middle East, Formosa and Red China), Business and Industry, Labor, Political Campaign, Legal Speaking, Education, and Religion.

The Introductions to earlier volumes (for example, the 1948-1949 edition) have listed alternate classifications based on speaking occasions and types, such as those before Congress, on the political stump, at labor gatherings, in the court room, at university and other educational meetings, on ceremonial occasions, and before religious groups; introductions of speakers; radio and television broadcasts.

Selection of speeches. The editor in each volume has disclaimed his selection as the "best" of the thousands of important speeches of the year. As he has previously put it, "he does attempt to single out those addresses that assume importance because of their ideas, organization, language, and delivery," and their social force in relation to major events and trends. The attempt is made to interpret the contemporary situations that affect or partly explain the American mind and conduct of today.

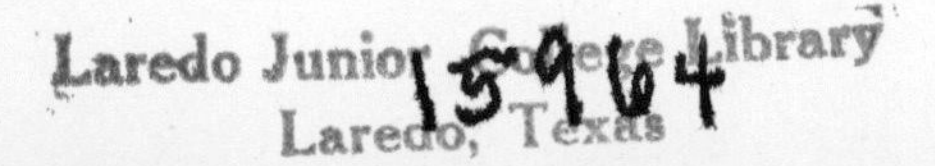

Introductions to the volumes. The Introduction to each of the twenty-two volumes deals with some phase of the methods of communication, or, as in the case of the present volume, a review of the leading movements of the preceding twelve months in their relation to significant speakers and speeches.

Introduction to each speech. A short introduction to each speech is included. One or more phases of the background and occasion, ideas, organization, language, audience appeals, the speaker's personality and delivery, and the immediate results of the speech are treated—to invite the reader to a more complete analysis and criticism of the speech.

Speech content. Complete speeches are given wherever practicable. Especially long speeches (e.g., some of those before the United States Senate) have been reprinted only in part.

Table of Contents and Cumulative Author Index. These twenty-two volumes with their individual contents and the Cumulative Author Index provide a reconstruction of the important events of American political, economic and cultural history and affairs since 1937.

Biographical notes. A brief biographical note concerning each speaker is given in the Appendix. It is assumed that such items will lead the reader to other sources for a full review of the speaker's career.

A reference source. This volume with its predecessors is a reference source, useful for the subject matter of these speeches since 1937 and for the information about the speakers and their methods. Each volume, in addition to its use as a library reference work, should aid school and college students of discussion and debate, public speaking, the history and criticism of American public address, and the social sciences.

The editor is grateful to the various speakers and publishers for their cooperation in providing authentic texts and for their permission for these reprints. Special acknowledgment is made in each case.

The editor appreciates the cooperation of several university libraries and their staffs, including those at the State University of Iowa, University of Missouri, Florida State University, University of Mississippi, University of Washington (Seattle), and Southern Illinois University. At this last-named library the present volume was completed.

A. CRAIG BAIRD

May 1959

CONTENTS

Education

Religion

INTRODUCTION

Speechmaking in the United States in 1958 and early 1959 was heavily affected by the political, military, and cultural events and trends of the year. Important speakers initiated policies and ideas that no doubt affected these problems and the solutions attempted. This interaction of social history and public address was constant. Each area of public speaking — congressional, political, industrial and professional, educational, religious, and ceremonial—whether by radio, television, or otherwise—closely reflected the major currents of American attitudes and decisions.

Speechmaking and International Affairs

On October 4, 1957, with the launching of the Soviet's Sputnik I, came the space age. Quickly followed another Sputnik and early in the new year the American earth satellites. Later came the Russian satellite that moved into the solar system. These vehicles in orbit evoked overnight and in the succeeding months of 1958 and 1959 nation-wide speechmaking. Americans engaged in self-indictment of our scientific tardiness and demanded dramatic action. What were the implications, it was asked, of these space achievements for world progress or for world destruction? Face-to-face debates and widely broadcast speeches focused on the issues raised by these earth moons and this Russian solar "planet."

Control of Nuclear Testing and Production

Should testing of nuclear weapons be prohibited by international agreement? Senator Hubert Humphrey on February 4, argued on the Senate floor, with much eloquence, that an agreement for such suspension with an inspection system was needed. Senator Styles Bridges, also speaking in the Senate, was skeptical of a Russian approval of foolproof inspection with adequate safeguards.

Dr. Harrison Brown, of the California Institute of Technology, spoke on March 9, for abandonment of the tests. Dr. Edward Teller, director of the University of California radiation laboratory, speaking before the subcommittee on disarmament of the Senate Committee on Foreign Relations, on April 16, contended that the stopping of tests and production would seriously weaken this country in the relative number and quality of weapons. Said he, "The Russians are developing the war machine faster than we are." Thus the sharp debate on the problem of the control of production and testing of nuclear weapons continued into the summer.

At Geneva international scientists worked on the problem and after secret talks announced on August 21 that nuclear tests could be effectively policed. The United States stated that its tests would be tentatively halted for one year and called for the Soviets to join with Great Britain and the United States in deliberations at Geneva on the problem, starting on October 31. Military and scientific experts, nevertheless, continued to be outspoken in their criticism of such deliberations. Senator Humphrey, in January 1959, after his return from Russia, continued to argue for such agreement despite the "new scientific data."

National Defense Organization

How should the Pentagon be reorganized to speed up our nuclear power development? On April 3 President Eisenhower gave to Congress his program for reorganizing the United States military establishment. The plan called for strengthening the authority of the Defense secretary, centralizing the Defense department under him, and downgrading the individual armed services. Strong opposition immediately developed. Representative Carl Vinson, for example, speaking in the House, denounced the plan as providing for a "man on horseback" who would dominate the military arm. President Eisenhower answered in a nationwide radio-television broadcast on April 17; speaking in an address at the joint luncheon of the American Society of Newspaper Editors and the International Press Institute, in Washington, the President pleaded for "maximum strength and minimum cost." General Maxwell Taylor defended the plea, as did Senator Stuart Symington, on April 20, and especially Secretary of Defense Neil McElroy, on April 22. Alexander de Seversky, consultant to the United States air forces, argued at that time before the Memphis chapter of the United States branch of the English-Speaking Union that "the reason we have reached a state of military inferiority vis-à-vis Russia is *not* that there is anything wrong with the American scientific creative genius, but that our talent is condemned by military orthodoxy to labor within the confines of an outmoded, fallacious framework."

In July, Congress, after prolonged Senate and House debate, gave the President the defense reorganization plan in substantially the form he wanted. Objectionable provisions however remained, such as the requirement that the Defense secretary exercise his authority through the respective service secretaries. The "czarist" factors were curtailed.

Foreign Aid

The Administration asked for foreign aid of $3.9 billion to begin July 1, 1958. Authorization for the program quickly passed Congress, with little reduction from that figure. The issue came at the second stage—the appropriation.

The House voted 253 to 126 for a bill cut by the House committee to $3 billion. The Senate vote raised this amount by several hundred millions, but after conferences to adjust differences, the emerging bill provided some $3 billion, slightly more than for the year before. This bill was at every step accompanied by vigorous debate.

Reciprocal Trade Agreements

The reciprocal trade agreements acts, adopted first in 1934 and yearly renewed, expired on June 30, 1958. The President asked for extension of the trade act for five years, with added power to cut tariffs up to 25 per cent. Congressional opposition was strong.

The House passed the bill after agreeing to an amendment that would allow Congress, by a two-thirds vote, to overrule the

President if he rejected a commission recommendation. Influential in the outcome were probably the long series of cross-country speeches by such legislators as Congressman A. S. J. Carnahan of Missouri; the decisive arguments by Eric Johnston, formerly president of the United States Chamber of Commerce; and the addresses of Clarence Randall, formerly president of Inland Steel.

The Middle East, Egypt, and Lebanon

The cold war of 1957 continued to agitate the Middle East during 1958 and early 1959. The Soviet propaganda machine working double time early in 1958 helped Russia to establish herself firmly in the power vacuum created by the withdrawal of France and Great Britain.

Lebanon became the center of the storm in May, June, and July, when a military group overthrew the royal regime of pro-Western Iraq, and President Chamoun of Lebanon called for American military support to protect his regime against "massive infiltration" from Syria. On July 15 President Eisenhower sent troops into Lebanon. The next day Britain followed with forces into Jordan. After much diplomatic sparring in the Security Council of the United Nations, the debate shifted to the General Assembly. The question was, Should American troops be ordered out of Lebanon and the British Army out of Jordan?

On Wednesday, August 13, President Eisenhower presented before the Assembly, and by radio and television to the United States and to the world, a United States program for the Middle East. American opinion almost solidly applauded the Eisenhower address as one of the best of his presidential career in its content, persuasiveness, and well-controlled delivery. His dramatic role before the eighty-one nations no doubt was a factor in the sudden assembly vote, 80 to 0, on August 21, to adopt the Arab League resolution. This resolution called on the members of the League to observe the pledge of non-interference in one another's internal affairs and requested that the General Assembly uphold the purposes and principles of the charter in relation to Lebanon and Jordan, thereby facilitating the early withdrawal of foreign troops.

For the time, American and world debate and United Nations Assembly action staved off a possible third world war threat in the Arab region. Instantly, however, a major conflict arose in the Far East.

Formosa and Red China

Red Chinese bombardment of the Nationalist off-shore island of Quemoy opened on August 23 and continued uninterruptedly into 1959.

On September 11, in the face of much American criticism of this country's defense of Quemoy, President Eisenhower gave a radio and television address in which he served notice to Peiping that the United States regarded Quemoy as our vital interest; in this speech the President pleaded for a negotiated settlement.

Much heated debate ensued in the General Assembly and elsewhere. The Assembly grappled with the old question of whether Red China should be seated. United States Ambassador Henry Cabot Lodge, Jr., on September 22, warned that the Chinese were "rapidly shooting themselves and shooting the world" out of any reasonable settlement of the dispute. Soviet Foreign Minister Gromyko spoke before Lodge and after him in uncompromising terms. The Assembly voted 44 to 28 against seating the Chinese Communists.

Secretary of State John Foster Dulles, on September 25, in a major speech before the Far East-America Council of Commerce and Industry in New York City, declared that the Communist challenge to the principle that armed force should not be used to combat aggression was involved. Said he, "We would find acceptable any arrangement that . . . did not involve surrender to force or threat of force." He followed on December 6 with perhaps his most important speech of 1958, on the same Red Chinese issue.

Speechmaking and Domestic Issues

Business and Industry

For the first time since 1944-1945, inflation and deflation became central problems. By the beginning of 1958 the recession was well under way. Steel, automobiles, and other basic industries sharply reduced their output. The stock market lost billions in market values. By March 1958, more than five million were unemployed. The cost of American defense and oversold markets were allegedly major causes.

AFL-CIO President George Meany, the author of several outstanding speeches since his election to office, concluded in an address before the AFL-CIO in Washington that the statistics "indicate a continued deepening of the recession" and "offer not a single ray of sunshine."

All was not gloom. Secretary of Labor James P. Mitchell, speaking on April 9 before the Advertising Club of New Jersey, avowed confidence in the economy and declared that those who despair "have lost faith in the ingenuity, the aggressiveness, and the ambition of every American citizen."

Vigorous pleas for major remedies were features of some addresses. Senate Majority Leader Lyndon Johnson of Texas, speaking in the Senate on April 19, said: "Personally, I don't intend to sit . . . [the recession] out." Sinclair Weeks, then Secretary of Commerce, spoke of the "ballyhoo of manufactured gloom."

Former President Harry S. Truman, addressing World War II veterans on April 1 with his old-time platform ardor, declared that "the recession is threatening the free world's security. . . . When our country is in peril . . . it is better to take too much action than too little." Two days later, before the House Banking and Currency Committee, he advocated a $5 billion tax reduction for middle- and lower-income families.

In April the decline leveled off. Truman in a New York speech proclaimed that the Administration was leading the nation to "bust," but Vice President Nixon countered in a New York speech before the American Newspaper Publishers Association, on April 24, that "we can state this one conclusion categorically: There will be no depression in the United States."

By June and early July, the signs of recovery were unmistakable. Democratic orators here and there continued to feature the recession, appealing to the army of workers still unemployed in Detroit and elsewhere. But evidence of prosperity mounted. By August, economists and others were speaking out against the rising tide of inflation. Steel and aluminum prices were upgraded. The Federal deficit was estimated at $12 billion, and an increase in the statutory debt limit to $288 billion was voted by Congress, presumably with inflationary results; and stock prices on the New York exchange were moving vigorously up—a sure indication of expected inflation.

Roger Blough, chairman of the board of U.S. Steel, speaking on September 15, placed the chief blame for inflation on labor's successful drives for higher wages.

Labor

Labor leaders George Meany, Walter Reuther of the United Automobile Workers of America, James B. Carey of the United Electrical, Radio, and Machine Workers, and David J. MacDonald of the United Steelworkers of America were all active speakers for labor in their respective organizations. Each denounced labor corruption and pleaded for high ethical standards in unionism. Each addressed his union at its annual convention and mapped out lines of labor philosophy and strategy. Meany, speaking on American labor and international affairs before the Commonwealth Club of California at San Francisco on April 23, defended unions as "the mortal enemies of dictatorship and injustice."

McDonald, at Atlantic City in September, opened the biennial convention of his union with oratorical language and unusually good speaking power (he is a former teacher of public speaking). Said he, "I say to you delegates if you want your union to be clean and strong, don't leave it up to the 'Great White Father' as I am now being called in the South." Earlier he had given a more statesmanlike address on "Labor's Responsibility for Human Rights."

The issue of union corruption carried on from the preceding year when James Hoffa replaced David Beck of the International Brotherhood of Teamsters and that union was expelled from the AFL-CIO. The Senate Select Committee on Improper Activities in the Labor or Management Field, with Senator John McClellan of Arkansas as chairman, continued to cross-examine Hoffa and other unionists.

The McClellan hearings were paralleled by vigorous congressional debate on legislation for labor reform. The Senate, after vigorous argument introduced by Senator John Kennedy of Massachusetts on June 12, passed a comprehensive bill in June—the Kennedy-Ives bill. At the end of July, however, the House killed the legislation. The political parties blamed each other for the failure to legislate in an area in which extremely unsavory practices had been revealed. Senator Kennedy charged that business groups headed by the National Association of Manufacturers had killed the bill "by misleading attacks."

Walter Reuther's public speaking as well as his prolonged conference talking related directly to the negotiations between the United Auto Workers and the Ford, General Motors, and Chrysler companies. After weeks of discussion across the tables and public comment by both company executives and Reuther, the new contracts were concluded with moderate wage increases not calculated to trigger sharp increases in the national cost of living.

Political Campaign

With congressional campaigns in every state and with "right-to-work" legislation proposed in six, the usual amount of sharp political campaign oratory and debate developed. Many free-swinging exchanges between gubernatorial and congressional candidates or their supporters ensued. The issues, state or national, were in most states not clearly defined. In New York State, Nelson A. Rockefeller, Republican candidate for governor, and Averell Harriman, up for reelection as a Democrat, spoke often, but without important contributions to significant American political address. The victorious Rockefeller, however, on January 1, 1959, gave a highly impressive inaugural address at Albany.

During the final two weeks of the campaign, President Eisenhower, Vice President Nixon, former President Harry S. Truman, and former candidate Adlai E. Stevenson, among others, injected much life into the campaign.

The Eisenhower political talks were perhaps the most skilled by the President and his political writers since the 1952 campaign. And Vice President Nixon was his old debating self with his direct thrusts at his opponents and his lively platform and television personality. He covered many states with keynote addresses, speaking, for example, at Columbus, Ohio, Indianapolis, Los Angeles, San Francisco, Baltimore, and in the agricultural centers of the Midwest. His themes were essentially those of his campaign of 1956—peace, prosperity, and progress.

Truman, too, carried on with his traditional fire, sarcasm, and bluntness. Wherever he spoke, down East or in the Middle West, he won constant headlines and large applause from his followers. He chided the Republicans who were running against "the Missouri farmer like they did in 1948." Senator Hubert Humphrey of Minnesota also proved an aggressive platform persuader for the Democrats, as did Senators Lyndon Johnson of Texas and George Smathers of Florida, in their southland appearances.

The "right-to-work" bills up for voter approval in Ohio, Kansas, Colorado, Idaho, Washington, and California found many voters crossing party lines in the arguments for and against the closed shop and the application of the Taft-Hartley Law.

Legal Speaking and the Little Rock Case

The Supreme Court convened on August 28, in an extraordinary session to hear oral arguments concerning the appeal of the Little Rock, Arkansas, school board for a delay in the integration of Central High School in that city.

Thurgood Marshall, attorney for the National Association for the Advancement of Colored People, who had successfully argued the original integration case before the court in 1954, appealed to the court to void a Court of Appeals stay and to overturn the suspension order which prohibited seven Negro children from enrolling. Richard C. Butler, the school board attorney, poised, systematic in his statement, called for time to work things out. J. Lee Rankin, United States Solicitor General, as a friend of the court, spoke eloquently against any delay.

The Justices themselves participated vigorously in the discussion, with frequent interruptions of the speakers, especially of Butler. The issues raised were: Can states or their officials challenge the authority of the Supreme Court? Can integration be suspended without flouting the concept of "deliberate speed"?

Oral arguments followed again on September 11. On the next day, Chief Justice Warren read the unanimous decision against delay in integration.

Senator Herman Talmadge of Georgia spoke bitterly of the Court's decision: "A second reconstruction of the South is in full swing backed by troops and bayonets." Senator Richard Russell, also of Georgia, said that "a great national tragedy impends." Other southern orators joined in the condemnation of Justice Warren and the Supreme Court.

Education

The advent of the nuclear age called for radical review of the American educational system. Where, the public asked, were the future scientists and technicians to come from? Were the schools doing their job? Were they soft on hard subjects and geared to "Life Adjustment" and fringe studies?

S. Scott Fletcher, president of the Fund for Adult Education of the Ford Foundation, before the Oklahoma Adult Education Association, on January 7, 1958, stressed the "battle of the curriculum." It should take account of the need for "partnership between educators of adults and mature learners."

Admiral H. G. Rickover, at Brooklyn Polytechnic Institute, on April 19, denounced the policy of equal treatment of all students in the name of democracy. In this speech, as in many others, he scorned "trivial" courses and demanded a return to the basic arts and sciences.

Francis O. Wilcox, Assistant Secretary of State for International Organization Affairs, logical in his analysis of the problem and forthright in his delivery of a speech at the State University of Iowa on June 13, denied that education in a free society should operate in the Soviet manner.

United States Commissioner of Education Lawrence G. Derthick in a speech at Chicago on March 5, and in a similar speech on June 16, discussed the Russian race for knowledge and also called for a modified but balanced American curriculum. Former Harvard President James B. Conant, in discussing the important role of education after high school before the Centennial Convention of the National Education Association at Philadelphia on July 3, expounded at length the proposition that "all educated Americans must have knowledge of the complexities of Western political and economic life," and that this education must be both political education and the individual and professional education of the youth. Dr. George S. Counts, the noted educator and author, in lectures across the nation in early July, warned against succumbing to a system imitative of that of Russia.

Significant also were the addresses of Harry S. Ashmore, editor of the *Arkansas Gazette,* at Washington University, St. Louis, on the problems of integration; of Erwin Canham, editor of the *Christian Science Monitor,* at the dedication of the National Education Association building in Washington, D.C., in February 1959; and of Robert Blakely, vice president of the Fund for Adult Education, with his plea for "education for multiple leadership," before the 1958 Conference on Continuing Education, at Michigan State University.

Senator J. William Fulbright of Arkansas, speaking before the Senate on several occasions during this period, indicted the American people and our educational standards and methods. His speeches before the Senate on January 23 and August 21, 1958, were outstanding.

President Grayson Kirk of Columbia University, at Smith College, on February 22; Senator Frank Church of Idaho, one of the more articulate and all-around debaters among younger senators, before the American Association of School Administrators, at San Francisco, on March 9; Representative Carroll Reece of Tennessee, before Congress, on June 11; President Virgil Hancher, of the Iowa State University, former university debater and orator, and later a seasoned speaker before many educational gatherings—these distinguished speakers also led in the oral analysis and discussion of the education issue.

The national high school discussion topic for the year was whether the United States should adopt the leading features of the British, French, or Soviet educational systems.

Commemorative Speaking

Outstanding among the commemorative, dedicatory, and similar speech types were those delivered by former President Herbert Hoover. His address at Valley Forge ceremonies on February 22, rated high by television and face-to-face listeners, as well as by the press, was a modification of one he gave there twenty-seven years before. The former President, lacking one month of eighty-four years, also spoke with notable clarity, logic, and appeal, on July 4, at the Brussels Exposition. (President Eisenhower had appointed him special envoy of the United States to the Fair.) Hoover followed this address with one on July 5 to the Belgian people, on "Hoover Day in Belgium." Both speeches in Belgium were widely acclaimed.

Eric Sevareid broadcast from Paris, on August 29, his farewell view of the current state of European attitudes and temper.

Radio-Television Speaking

Edward R. Murrow, with his "Small World" and similar television programs, remained the most noteworthy of the commentators who aimed at public information and interpretation of national and world problems. Similar television personalities included John Daly, Eric Sevareid, Howard K. Smith, and Alistair Cooke.

Religious Speaking

American clergymen applied fervor and sermonic skills to influence American religious attitudes and programs. Billy Graham with his campaigns in San Francisco and elsewhere continued to be the headline evangelistic preacher of the period. The death of Pope Pius XII evoked many tributes both within and without churches of all denominations and produced extended commentaries over the radio and television.

Outstanding among religious speakers were many laymen—among them W. H. Stringer, a *Christian Science Monitor* journalist, who spoke at the University of Louisiana on February 24—and such clergymen as Norman Vincent Peale, Bishop Fulton J. Sheen, Francis Cardinal Spellman, Joseph R. Sizoo, Ralph Sockman, Reinhold Niebuhr, and Bishop Richard Emrich, who continued to have wide audiences within their denominations and to preach to thousands of radio-television hearer-observers.

INTERNATIONAL POLICIES AND ATTITUDES

A PLAN FOR PEACE IN LEBANON[1]

DWIGHT D. EISENHOWER[2]

President Dwight D. Eisenhower gave this address before the General Assembly of the United Nations, on Wednesday, August 13, 1958. He faced the delegates from eighty-one nations in this emergency session. It was the President's first appearance there since his "Atoms for Peace" proposal in 1953.[3]

The Middle East crisis involving Lebanon, Jordan, and Iraq developed on July 14, when the pro-Western government of Iraq was overthrown. At the request of the Lebanese government, the United States sent a military force into Lebanon (July 15) to prevent a similar coup there and the British moved into Jordan (July 17). Moscow warned that it would not be "indifferent" to these military moves, and vetoed a resolution in the Security Council calling for the United Nations to take over the job of policing the Middle East. The United States then announced that it would carry its plea to the General Assembly. Premier Khrushchev countered by calling for a summit meeting at Geneva to avoid "the world's greatest catastrophe." In the ensuing diplomatic exchanges, the merits and demerits of a summit conference were bandied back and forth.

President Eisenhower, on August 1, announced that the main problem of the Middle East was "indirect aggression" and therefore was the responsibility of the United Nations Security Council. This nation, he said, would seek a special Council meeting on or about August 12. With Khrushchev's rejection of the proposal and with the chances of the summit conference gone, the issue shifted to the General Assembly.

That body convened on August 8 and agreed to grapple with the problem, beginning on August 13. Any constructive move would require a two-thirds vote—with little prospect that any bloc could muster such a majority.

This was the situation when President Eisenhower spoke. He denounced the practice of aggressive powers' confronting small nations with the apparent choice between surrender or war. He defended the Anglo-

[1] Text "as actually delivered" furnished by James C. Hagerty, press secretary to President Eisenhower, with permission for this reprint. For the text see also the New York *Times*, August 14, 1958, p6.

[2] For biographical note, see Appendix.

[3] See *Representative American Speeches: 1953-54*, p22-32.

American intervention in Lebanon and Jordan and outlined a six-point program for solving the problem.

After much discussion in the Assembly and behind-the-scenes negotiation, the issue was resolved on August 20, when ten Arab powers, the Arab League with Tunisia and Morocco, presented a resolution that they had secretly drafted. Their proposal, which took the Assembly by complete surprise, called on the Arab states to observe the pledge of noninterference in one another's internal affairs contained in the League Pact and requested the UN Secretary General to "facilitate the early withdrawal of foreign troops." The resolution was unanimously approved.

As 1958 ended the British and American troops had withdrawn, and peace—at least on the surface—displaced the war drums.

The President read his nine-page speech in a firm voice that hesitated only three or four times. No applause interrupted, and "the only sounds were the click of camera shutters and the rustle of pages turned by those following his text." The talk was simultaneously translated into French, Russian, Spanish, and Chinese.

The principal architect of the President's General Assembly speech, according to a report in the New York *Times,* August 18, was C. D. Jackson of Time Inc., formerly the President's adviser on psychological warfare.

Congress was enthusiastic about Eisenhower's address. Senators and representatives were almost unanimous in their spontaneous bipartisan support of his plan for the Middle East. Within two hours hundreds of telegrams of congratulation poured in and it was evident that Americans who had heard the proceedings over television and radio were equally enthusiastic. The President had effectively identified this nation as the champion of peaceful development of the Middle East. And in his success the failure of Russia as the sponsor of unrest was obvious.

Mr. President, Mr. Secretary General, Members of the General Assembly, and Guests:

First, may I express my gratitude for the generosity of your welcome.

It has been almost five years since I had the honor of addressing this Assembly. I then spoke of atomic power and urged that we should find the way by which the miraculous inventiveness of man should not be dedicated to his death but consecrated to his life. Since then great strides have been taken in the use of atomic energy for peaceful purposes. Tragically, little has been done to eliminate the use of atomic and nuclear power for weapons purposes.

That is a danger.

That danger in turn gives rise to another danger—the danger that nations under aggressive leadership will seek to exploit man's horror of war by confronting the nations, particularly small nations, with an apparent choice between supine surrender, or war.

This tactic reappeared during the recent Near East crisis.

Some might call it "ballistic blackmail."

In most communities it is illegal to cry "fire" in a crowded assembly. Should it not be considered serious international misconduct to manufacture a general war scare in an effort to achieve local political aims?

Pressures such as these will never be successfully practiced against America, but they do create dangers which could affect each and every one of us. That is why I have asked for the privilege of again addressing you.

The immediate reason is two small countries—Lebanon and Jordan.

The cause is one of universal concern.

The lawful and freely elected government of Lebanon, feeling itself endangered by civil strife fomented from without, sent the United States a desperate call for instant help. We responded to that call.

On the basis of that response an effort has been made to create a war hysteria. The impression is sought to be created that if small nations are assisted in their desire to survive, that endangers the peace.

This is truly an "upside down" portrayal. If it is made an international crime to help a small nation maintain its independence, then indeed the possibilities of conquest are unlimited. We will have nullified the provision of our Charter which recognizes the inherent right of collective self-defense. We will let loose forces that could generate great disasters.

The United Nations has, of course, a primary responsibility to maintain not only international peace but also "security." But we must not evade a second fact, namely, that in the circumstances of the world since 1945, the United Nations has sometimes been blocked in its attempt to fulfill that function.

Respect for the liberty and freedom of all nations has always been a guiding principle of the United States. This respect has

been consistently demonstrated by our unswerving adherence to the principles of the Charter, particularly in its opposition to aggression, direct or indirect. Sometimes we have made that demonstration in terms of collective measures called for by the United Nations. Sometimes we have done so pursuant to what the Charter calls "the inherent right of collective self-defense."

I recall the moments of clear danger we have faced since the end of the Second World War—Iran, Greece and Turkey, the Berlin blockade, Korea, the Straits of Taiwan.

A common principle guided the position of the United States on all of these occasions. That principle was that aggression, direct or indirect, must be checked before it gathered sufficient momentum to destroy us all—aggressor and defender alike.

It was this principle that was applied once again when the urgent appeals of the governments of Lebanon and Jordan were answered.

I would be less than candid if I did not tell you that the United States reserves, within the spirit of this Charter, the right to answer the legitimate appeal of any nation, particularly small nations.

I doubt that a single free government in all the world would willingly forgo the right to ask for help if its sovereignty were imperiled.

But I must again emphasize that the United States seeks always to keep within the spirit of the Charter.

Thus when President Truman responded in 1947 to the urgent plea of Greece, the United States stipulated that our assistance would be withdrawn whenever the United Nations felt that its action could take the place of ours.

Similarly, when the United States responded to the urgent plea of Lebanon, we went at once to the Security Council and sought United Nations assistance for Lebanon so as to permit the withdrawal of United States forces.

United Nations action would have been taken, and United States forces already withdrawn, had it not been for two resolutions, one proposed by the United States, the other proposed by the government of Japan, failed to pass because of one negative vote—a veto.

But nothing that I have said is to be construed as indicating that I regard the status quo as sacrosanct. Change is indeed the law of life and of progress. But when change reflects the will of the people, then change can and should be brought about in peaceful ways.

In this context the United States respects the right of every Arab nation of the Near East to live in freedom without domination from any source, far or near.

In the same context, we believe that the Charter of the United Nations places on all of us certain solemn obligations. Without respect for each other's sovereignty and the exercise of great care in the means by which new patterns of international life are achieved, the projection of the peaceful vision of the Charter would become a mockery.

II

Let me turn now specifically to the problem of Lebanon.

When the United States military assistance began moving into Lebanon, I reported to the American people that we had immediately reacted to the plea of Lebanon because the situation was such that only prompt action would suffice.

I repeat to you the solemn pledge I then made: Our assistance to Lebanon has but one single purpose—that is the purpose of the Charter and of such historic resolutions of the United Nations as the "Essentials for Peace" Resolution of 1949 and the "Peace through Deeds" Resolution of 1950. These denounce, as a form of aggression and as an international crime, the fomenting of civil strife in the interest of a foreign power.

We want to prevent that crime—or at least prevent its having fatal consequences. We have no other purpose whatsoever.

The United States troops will be totally withdrawn whenever this is requested by the duly constituted government of Lebanon or whenever, through action by the United Nations or otherwise, Lebanon is no longer exposed to the original danger.

It is my earnest hope that this Assembly, free of the veto, will consider how it can assure the continued independence and integrity of Lebanon. Thus the political destiny of the Lebanese people will continue to lie in their own hands.

The United States delegation will support measures to this end.

III

Another urgent problem is Jordan.

If we do not act promptly in Jordan a further dangerous crisis may result, for the method of indirect aggression discernible in Jordan may lead to conflicts endangering the peace.

We must recognize that peace in this area is fragile, and we must also recognize that the end of peace in Jordan could have consequences of a far-reaching nature. The United Nations has a particular responsibility in this matter, since it sponsored the Palestine armistice agreements upon which peace in the area rests and since it also sponsors the care of the Palestine refugees.

I hope that this Assembly will be able to give expression to the interest of the United Nations in preserving the peace in Jordan.

IV

There is another matter which this Assembly should face in seeking to promote stability in the Near East. That is the question of inflammatory propaganda. The United Nations Assembly has on three occasions—in 1947, 1949 and 1950—passed resolutions designed to stop the projecting of irresponsible broadcasts from one nation into the homes of citizens of another nation, thereby "fomenting civil strife and subverting the will of the people in any state." That is stated in the language of the resolution. We all know that these resolutions have recently been violated in many directions in the Near East.

If we, the United States, are one of those who have been at fault we stand ready to be corrected.

I believe that this Assembly should reaffirm its enunciated policy and should consider means for monitoring the radio broadcasts directed across national frontiers in the troubled Near East area. It should then examine the complaints from these nations which consider their national security jeopardized by external propaganda.

V

The countries of this area should also be freed from armed pressure and infiltration coming across their borders. When such interference threatens they should be able to get from the United Nations prompt and effective action to help safeguard their independence. This requires that adequate machinery be available to make the United Nations presence manifest in the area of trouble.

Therefore I believe that this Assembly should take action looking toward the creation of a standby United Nations Peace Force. The need for such a Force is being clearly demonstrated by recent events involving imminent danger to the integrity of two of our members.

I understand that this general subject is to be discussed at the thirteenth General Assembly and that our distinguished Secretary General has taken an initiative in this matter. Recent events clearly demonstrate that this is a matter for urgent and positive action.

VI

Now I have proposed four areas of action for the consideration of the Assembly—in respect to Lebanon, to Jordan, to subversive propaganda and a standby United Nations force. These measures, basically, are designed to do one thing: to preserve the right of a nation and its people to determine their own destiny, consistent with the obligation to respect the rights of others.

This clearly applies to the great surge of Arab nationalism.

Let me state the position of my country unmistakably. The peoples of the Arab nations of the Near East clearly possess the right of determining and expressing their own destiny. Other nations should not interfere so long as this expression is found in ways compatible with international peace and security.

However, here as in other areas we have an opportunity to share in a great international task. That is the task of assisting the peoples of that area, under programs which they may desire, to make further progress toward the goals of human welfare they have set for themselves. Only on the basis of progressing economies can truly independent governments sustain themselves.

This is a real challenge to the Arab people and to all of us.

To help the Arab countries fulfill their aspirations, here is what I propose:

First—that consultations be immediately undertaken by the Secretary General with the Arab nations of the Near East to ascertain whether an agreement can be reached to establish an Arab development institution on a regional basis.

Second—that these consultations consider the composition and the possible functions of a regional Arab development institution, whose task would be to accelerate progress in such fields as industry, agriculture, water supply, health and education among others.

Third—other nations and private organizations which might be prepared to support this institution should also be consulted at an appropriate time.

Should the Arab States agree on the usefulness of such a soundly organized regional institution, and should they be prepared to support it with their own resources, the United States would also be prepared to support it.

The institution would be set up to provide loans to the Arab States as well as the technical assistance required in the formulation of development projects.

The institution should be governed by the Arab States themselves.

This proposal for a regional Arab development institution can, I believe, be realized on a basis which would attract international capital, both public and private.

I also believe that the best and quickest way to achieve the most desirable result would be for the Secretary General to make two parallel approaches. First to consult with the Arab States of the Near East to determine an area of agreement. Then to invite the International Bank for Reconstruction and Development, which has vast experience in this field, to make available its facilities for the planning of the organizational and operational techniques needed to establish the institution on its progressive course.

I hope it is clear that I am not suggesting a position of leadership for my own country in the work of creating such an institution. If this institution is to be a success, the function of leadership must belong to the Arab States themselves.

I would hope that high on the agenda of this institution would be action to meet one of the major challenges of the Near East, the great common shortage—water.

Much scientific and engineering work is already under way in the field of water development. For instance atomic isotopes now permit us to chart the courses of the great underground rivers. The new horizons are opening in the desalting of water. The ancient problem of water is on the threshold of solution. Energy, determination and science will carry it over that threshold.

Another great challenge that faces the area is disease.

Already there is substantial effort among the peoples and governments of the Near East to conquer disease and disability. But much more remains to be done.

The United States is prepared to join with other governments and the World Health Organization in an all-out, joint attack on preventable disease in the Near East.

But to see the desert blossom again and preventable disease conquered is only a first step. As I look into the future I see the emergence of modern Arab states that would bring to this century contributions surpassing those we cannot forget from the past. We remember that Western arithmetic and algebra owe much to Arabic mathematicians and that much of the foundation of the world's medical science and astronomy was laid by Arab scholars. Above all, we remember that three of the world's great religions were born in the Near East.

But a true Arab renaissance can only develop in a healthy human setting. Material progress should not be an overriding objective in itself. It is an important condition for achieving higher human, cultural and spiritual objectives.

But I repeat, if this vision of the modern Arab community is to come to life, the goals must be Arab goals.

VII

With the assistance of the United Nations, the countries of the Near East now have a unique opportunity to advance, in freedom, their security and their political and economic interests. If a plan for peace of the kind I am proposing can be carried forward, in a few short years we may be able to look back on the Lebanon and Jordan crises as the beginning of a great new prosperous era of Arab history.

But there is an important consideration which must remain in mind today and in the future.

If there is an end to external interference in the internal affairs of the Arab States of the Near East—

If an adequate United Nations Peace Force is in existence—

If a regional development institution exists and is at work on the basic projects and programs designed to lift the living standards of the area—

Then with this good prospect, and indeed as a necessary condition for its fulfillment, I hope and believe that the nations of the area, intellectually and emotionally, will no longer feel the need to seek national security through spiraling military build-ups. These lead not only to economic impotence but to war.

Perhaps the nations involved in the 1948 hostilities may, as a first step, wish to call for a United Nations study of the flow of heavy armaments to those nations. My country would be glad to support the establishment of an appropriate United Nations body to examine this problem. That body would discuss it individually with these countries and see what arms control arrangements could be worked out under which the security of all these nations could be maintained more effectively than under a continued wasteful, dangerous competition in armaments. I recognize that any such arrangements must reflect these countries' own views.

VIII

I have tried to present to you the framework of a plan for peace in the Near East. It would provide a setting of political order responsive to the rights of the people in each nation; which would avoid the dangers of a regional arms race; which would permit the peoples of the Near East to devote their energies wholeheartedly to the tasks of development and human progress in the widest sense.

It is important that the six elements of this program be viewed as a whole. They are:

(1) United Nations concern for Lebanon.

(2) United Nations measures to preserve peace in Jordan.

(3) An end to the fomenting from without of civil strife.

(4) A United Nations Peace Force.

(5) A regional economic development plan to assist and accelerate improvement in the living standards of the people in these Arab nations.

(6) Steps to avoid a new arms race spiral in the area.

To have solidity, the different elements of this plan for peace and progress should be considered and acted on together, as integral elements of a single concerted effort.

Therefore, I hope that this Assembly will seek simultaneously to set in motion measures that would create a climate of security in the Near East consonant with the principles of the United Nations Charter, and at the same time create the framework for a common effort to raise the standard of living of the Arab peoples.

IX

But the peoples of the Near East are not alone in their ambition for independence and development. We are living in a time when the whole world has become alive to the possibilities for modernizing their societies.

The American government has been steadily enlarging its allocations to foreign economic development in response to these world-wide hopes. We have joined in partnership with such groupings as the Organization of American States and the Colombo Plan; and we are working on methods to strengthen these regional arrangements. For example, in the case of the Organization of American States, we are consulting now with our sister republics of this hemisphere to strengthen its role in economic development. And the government of the United States has not been alone in supporting development efforts. The British Commonwealth, the countries of Western Europe, and Japan have all made significant contributions.

But in many parts of the world both geography and wise economic planning favor national rather than regional development programs. The United States will, of course, continue its firm support of such national programs. Only where the desire for a regional approach is clearly manifested and where the advantage of regional over national is evident will the United States change to regional methods.

The United States is proud of the scope and variety of its development activities throughout the world. Those who know our history will realize that this is no sudden, new policy of our government. Ever since its birth, the United States has gladly shared its wealth with others. This it has done without the thought of conquest or economic domination. After victory in two world wars and the expenditure of vast treasure there is no world map, either geographic or economic, on which anyone can find that the force of American arms or the power of the American Treasury has absorbed any foreign land or political or economic system. As we cherish our freedom, we believe in freedom for others.

X

The things I have talked about today are real and they await our grasp. Within the Near East and within this Assembly are the forces of good sense, of restraint, and of wisdom to make, with time and patience, a framework of political order and of peace in that region.

But we also know that all these possibilities are shadowed, all our hopes are dimmed, by the fact of the arms race in nuclear weapons—a contest which drains off our best talents and vast resources, straining the nerves of all our peoples.

As I look out on this Assembly, with so many of you representing new nations, one thought above all impresses me.

The world that is being remade on our planet is going to be a world of many mature nations. As one after another of these new nations moves through the difficult transition to modernization and learns the methods of growth, from this travail new levels of prosperity and productivity will emerge.

This world of individual nations is not going to be controlled by any one power or group of powers. This world is not going to be committed to any one ideology.

Please believe me when I say that the dream of world domination by one power or of world conformity is an impossible dream.

The nature of today's weapons, the nature of modern communications, and the widening circle of new nations make it plain that we must, in the end, be a world community of open societies.

And the concept of the open society is the ultimate key to a system of arms control we all can trust.

We must, then, seek with new vigor, new initiative, the path to a peace based on the effective control of armaments, on economic advancement and on the freedom of all peoples to be ruled by governments of their choice. Only thus can we exercise the full capacity God has given us to enrich the lives of the individual human beings who are our ultimate concern, our responsibility and our strength.

In this memorable task there lies enough work and enough reward to satisfy the energies and ambitions of all leaders, everywhere.

Thank you very much for your kind attention.

POLICY FOR THE FAR EAST [4]

John Foster Dulles [5]

The Honorable John Foster Dulles, then Secretary of State, addressed the California Chamber of Commerce at San Francisco, December 4, 1958, on United States policy for the Far East.

Preliminary to the exposition of his main theme, Mr. Dulles recapitulated the nation's record in checking Communist aggression by retaliatory power. He urged continued application of our strength and our will to make war "unprofitable" to the Soviets. He wished to protect and develop free from Communist domination the twenty-one nations that have emerged in the postwar period. For these young nations his was a proposal primarily for American political and economic support by investments and trade policies. He cited the evidence to prove his familiar dictum that "freedom is still a magnet that attracts."

This address on our Far East policies was comprehensive, factually supported, and persuasively phrased. Clearly Dulles was on the defensive against much American opinion favoring recognition of Red China—opinion held by those who indicted our Quemoy-Formosa stand.

Dulles spoke often in 1958, with some dozen major addresses to the American public and the world. In addition to traveling over the globe to meet constantly rising crises, he probably did more speaking during this period, despite his illness, than any other secretary of state in America's history.[6]

The resignation of the cancer-stricken Secretary in April 1959 evoked expressions of deep regret not only in the United States but throughout the Western world.

I always consider that United States foreign policy is designed to serve one of the basic purposes of our Constitution, to "secure the Blessings of Liberty to ourselves and our Posterity." There was a time when foreign policy played a relatively minor role in that great task. Today its role is major.

The world has been so shrunk by the developments of science and technology that events anywhere impinge on men

[4] Text supplied through the courtesy of Maurice S. Rice, Chief, Public Services Division, Department of State.

[5] For biographical note, see Appendix.

[6] For further comment on John Foster Dulles as a speaker, see the Cumulative Author Index for references to his speeches in earlier volumes.

everywhere. Furthermore, international communism, seeking its "one world," operates against us on a global basis.

Its leaders have always considered that the United States was the hardest nut for them to crack. They hope, however, to do so by first getting control of the rest of the world, leaving the United States so encircled and isolated and subject to such economic strangulation that, as Stalin put it, we will recognize that continuing struggle is hopeless and will "voluntarily" accept the Communist concept.

During the period preceding and following the Second World War international communism made immense gains in Europe and in Asia. Now it rules about 900 million people.

In recent years that expanding process has been checked. That has been the result of overall policies that I shall briefly recall before turning more particularly to the Pacific scene.

Retaliatory Power

It is our policy to check the Communist use or threat of force by having retaliatory power, and the will to use it, so that the Communist use of force would obviously be unprofitable to them.

I emphasize both the power and the will. One without the other is useless. Also, that will must be made sufficiently manifest that potential aggressors, when they make their calculations, will calculate that they could not aggress without disaster to themselves.

It is not pleasant to have to plan in these terms. But in the world as it is, there is no other way to peace and security for ourselves and for other parts of the endangered free world.

Forces-in-Being

It is, however, not enough merely to have great retaliatory striking power. It is necessary to have forces-in-being at endangered points. Nations which are in close proximity to powerful aggressive forces need the reassurance of some visible force within their own territory. They are not content to be wholly dependent upon forces and decisions elsewhere.

Furthermore, vast retaliatory power should not be, and will not be, invoked lightly. There must be an ability to oppose what may be limited probings in ways less drastic than general nuclear war.

A capacity quickly to help Lebanon; such power as was rapidly deployed in the Taiwan area; the presence of United States forces in such areas as Berlin, West Germany, and Korea —all contribute essentially to the peace and security of our own country.

Most of the "limited war" forces are contributed by our allies. For example, they contribute 80 per cent of the ground forces. We help to maintain and support these forces by supplying, where needed, military weapons and occasionally some financial support.

This is truly a system of "collective" security. It provides security both for the United States and for our allies.

Coping with Political and Economic Subversion

We also have policies to cope with the Communist tactics of political and economic subversion.

The former colonial areas have long been marked out as special prey for communism. Lenin taught that international communism should stimulate "nationalism" to the point of breaking, totally, political, economic, and cultural ties between the so-called "colonial and dependent areas" and the Western powers. Then, it was calculated, the new countries would become so dependent upon the Communist nations that the former colonial peoples could, as Lenin put it, be "amalgamated" into the Communist bloc.

That strategy is being actively pursued today, taking advantage of the liberating policies of the colonial powers.

During the postwar period twenty-one new nations have been granted political independence, and others are on the threshold of independence. International communism is striving to gain control of these new countries. Its efforts are reinforced by the rapid economic development going on within the existing Sino-Soviet orbit. There harsh discipline and extreme austerity extract rapid economic growth out of the people. The newly independent and the less developed countries see this growth and are told that with Communist help and guidance they could make the same progress. International communism is now in a position to supply many technicians and considerable amounts of economic aid to support its subversive program.

That means that these free nations which possess accumulated capital need to assist the less developed countries to carry out, in freedom, development programs. The peoples of the less developed countries must feel that they live in an environment that is made dynamic by forces that will lift them out of what, for most, has been a stagnant morass of poverty.

This task is, primarily, one for private capital and normal trade. But government must effectively supplement private efforts. When it does so, it is demonstrably acting to secure for us and our posterity the blessings of liberty.

If these new countries, representing much of Asia and Africa, fall to communism and if the same lure operates in Latin America, then international communism would have gone far to having the United States within the cruel clutch of its encirclement.

Demonstrating What Free Men Can Do

It is never sufficient to be defensive. Freedom must be a positive force that will penetrate.

Only individuals and free enterprise can impart that quality. In a struggle where individual freedom is the issue, government cannot carry all the responsibility. Governments of the free can do much. But the essential exponents of freedom are free people.

Our nation was founded as a great experiment in freedom. Our people were endowed with a sense of mission. As put in the opening paragraph of *The Federalist* papers, we hoped by our "conduct and example" to demonstrate to all the world the advantages of a free and self-governing society. And, in fact, we did just that.

When our nation was formed, the tide of despotism was high. We contributed largely to rolling it back. What we did became known as the "Great American Experiment," and it caught the imagination of men everywhere.

We must be imbued with that spirit and set that example. Freedom is still a magnet that attracts. Let me recall these facts:

> Of the Chinese Communist prisoners taken in Korea, two thirds rejected repatriation.
>
> From Communist China the people flee to Hong Kong and Macao.
>
> In Korea about 2 million have gone from the Communist north to the south.
>
> In Vietnam nearly 1 million went from the Communist north to the south.
>
> During the Hungarian rebellion, 200,000 escaped to freedom.
>
> In Germany over 3 million have gone from east to west.

Indeed, the evidence suggests a "law" of popular gravitation to democratic freedom.

Within the past five years there have been violent outbreaks in East Berlin, East Germany, Poland, Hungary, and Communist China.

Today the Soviet rulers threaten West Berlin. Why? It is because they are put on the defensive by the inspiring demonstration there of what free men can do.

Communist rulers have shown a formidable capacity to impose their rule. But, if free men will show the good fruits of freedom, the enslavers will always be on the defensive and will face the ultimate collapse of their system.

The Pacific and the Far East

Let me now turn to the Pacific and the Far East. I first mention certain aspects of the situation that are distinctive.

1. In Asia international communism now controls a great population and land mass represented by the China mainland, Tibet, North Korea, and North Vietnam.

2. The non-Communist countries are scattered about the rim of this great mass. For the most part they constitute separated insular or peninsular positions. Historically, they lack common ties; there is little sense of regional unity. As between some of the free Asian countries, there is antagonism.

3. The Communist regime in Peiping, closely leagued with Moscow, is bearing down hard on the free Asian countries with its massive weight of numbers, its rising military power, and its infiltration among overseas Chinese. They constitute a large and influential element in most of the free Asian countries. It penetrates labor unions, student groups, and left-wing political parties. It has an elaborate underground apparatus and extensive propaganda facilities.

4. Internally, Red China is feverishly imposing a communization program designed quickly to transform the Chinese nation into a great military and industrial power. The program involves human slavery and cruelty on a scale unprecedented in all world history. But it is producing material results.

5. The communization program inevitably creates widespread discontent. The dictators of that program, in order to divert hostility from themselves, pretend that their program is needed because the United States threatens to attack. They have launched a virulent "Hate America" campaign.

6. Of the eleven free Far Eastern countries, eight have gained their independence only since 1945. They inevitably lack experience in public administration. They are in an early stage of economic development. Their industries remain to be created. Their standards of living are low.

These conditions of the Far East are quite different from those of Western Europe, for example. There the free countries are contiguous; they have a similar culture; they are well developed economically.

Despite the differing circumstances that must always be taken into account, the basic principles which I have outlined are nevertheless applicable in the Far East and can preserve freedom there.

Collective Security Arrangements

We have developed collective security arrangements in the Far East to the maximum extent so far practical. Of these security arrangements the most significant is that created by the Southeast Asia Collective Defense Treaty. In addition, the United States has bilateral security arrangements with the Republics of the Philippines, Korea, and China and with Japan. We have a trilateral treaty with Australia and New Zealand.

The United States, in support of these collective defense treaties, maintains large mobile power, air and sea, in the Pacific, and some ground forces, particularly in Korea. These are part of a free-world defense network in the Far East involving some 1,750,000 troops, most of them battle-experienced. These forces deter, and can resist, Communist armed aggression. They are backed up by the retaliatory striking power of the United States, if this is needed.

There have been no Communist territorial gains in the Far East since 1954 when SEATO was formed and these bilateral treaties made.

The recent Communist show of force in the Taiwan area was for the avowed purpose of liquidating the government of the Republic of China and expelling the United States from the Western Pacific. It was pushed to the point of ascertaining whether the United States had the will to fight if challenged. We showed that will and avoided a loss which would have been not merely Quemoy but, ultimately, the entire free-world position in the Western Pacific.

U.S. Attitude Toward Chinese Communist Regime

In addition to contributing to military security, the United States promotes the general economic and political health of the free nations of the Far East. This is in accord both with our tradition and with our interest. Also we thereby combat the Chinese Communist tactics of subversion.

In this connection I should like to mention our attitude toward Communist China. I spoke of this rather fully in a talk which I made here in San Francisco in June of last year. What I now say is designed to supplement and not to subtract from what I then said.

Developments make it ever more clear that, if we were to grant political recognition to the Chinese Communist regime, that would be a well-nigh mortal blow to the survival of the non-Communist governments in the Far East. Such recognition and the seating of the Chinese Communists in the United Nations would so increase their prestige and influence in the Far East, and so dishearten our allies there, that the Communist subversive efforts would almost surely succeed.

Contrary arguments come largely from two sources. There are those who argue that, since the Chinese Communist regime exists and has power on the mainland, we ought to accord it political recognition.

There is, however, no principle of international law to this effect. Recognition is a privilege which can be accorded or withheld. There are several *de facto* regimes in the world that we do not recognize. We act, in these matters, as our national interest dictates.

The Chinese Communist regime is bitterly hostile to the United States. It is dedicated to expelling all our influence from the Western Pacific. It is determined to take over the free peoples and resources of the area. It violates all established principles of international law and of civilized conduct.

Why should we give aid and comfort to such a regime and to such policies?

Some argue we should recognize the Chinese Communist regime in the hope that large and profitable trade would follow. That is an illusion. The mainland of China has never been a large customer of the United States, and its trade is even more closely regimented under Communist rule.

The United States today is exporting to the non-Communist countries of the Far East at the rate of over $2.5 billion a year. This figure excludes the value of military items exported under our mutual security programs.

It is certain that, if the Communists should take over these free nations of the Far East, our trade with them would drastically shrink, as has been the case with our trade with the Soviet Union and its European satellites. We must also recall that, because Communist nations look on trade primarily as a political instrument, citizens of free nations can rarely engage in such trade profitably or safely.

Should we, then, in the quest of a few millions of dollars of unreliable trade with Communist China jeopardize exports of $2.5 billion?

We deal with the Chinese Communist regime wherever that is expedient. We do not pretend that it does not exist. We have been in almost constant negotiations with it for particular purposes, at Panmunjom, at the Geneva conference on Indo-China, in bilateral negotiations at Geneva and now at Warsaw.

But it is certain that diplomatic recognition of the Chinese Communist regime would gravely jeopardize the political, the economic, and the security interests of the United States. The Pacific instead of being, as it is today, a friendly body of water would in great part be dominated by hostile forces and our own defenses there would be driven back to or about our continental frontiers.

"Dumping" Practices

There is developing a special threat to free-world trade in the Far East. That is the "dumping" practice of Communist China. The Chinese mainland people desperately need for themselves all that they are capable of producing. But they are denied, so that the rulers may prosecute their expansionist designs.

When millions of Chinese are dying of starvation, rice is exported for political purposes.

Goods manufactured in China are being dumped in Southeast Asia at prices that disrupt normal trade. These include textiles, bicycles, sewing machines, fountain pens, and the like. This is particularly a present threat to the trade of Japan in South and Southeast Asia.

This problem as it arises in the Far East is one phase of the economic offensive now being initiated by the Sino-Soviet bloc. Your Government is intensively studying this problem. We have asked business people—some from the group I am addressing—

to study it. There is no doubt in my mind but what concrete measures will be needed to assure that in the face of this unfair competition free enterprise will continue to play its full role as a dynamic and expanding force in developing the economies of the free-world nations.

Preserving Chinese Culture

One essential sought by our Far Eastern policy is to assure that the Chinese Communists do not acquire, as an exclusive propaganda tool of their own, the prestige that attaches to Chinese culture. This prestige is great.

Chinese culture has ancient historic roots and is an influence today throughout the Far East. It derives from the family life, the veneration of the ancestor, and the training of youth to respect their parents. It comprehends the creation and admiration of what is beautiful in color, form, and arrangement. It stimulates and honors education in the broad humanitarian and philosophical sense of that word.

Today, on the mainland, not only Chinese culture but every aspect of human dignity is sought to be eradicated.

Under the Chinese Communist "commune" system, individuality and personality are brutally suppressed. The individual is valued, and allowed to survive, only as a laborer for the state. "All-purpose" workers, in blocs of tens of thousands, are herded into crude dormitories, with men and women largely segregated, and children placed in wholesale nurseries, so that the women can also be part of the slave labor force. The venerated graves of ancestors are everywhere being desecrated. The respected customs and beliefs of the people, the basic values of family life, education in the broad sense, the art of the beautiful are being obliterated in the name of the "great leap" decreed by Peiping.

It is important to all the world that Chinese culture be preserved. Fortunately there is a qualified custodian of that culture—the government of the Republic of China, with its present seat at Taipei.

A few weeks ago I went to Taipei to discuss the general situation with the President and other members of that government.

Out of that consultation came a declaration which is, I think, noteworthy. Let me read these passages:

> The government of the Republic of China declared its purpose to be a worthy representative of the Chinese people and to strive to preserve those qualities and characteristics which have enabled the Chinese to contribute so much of benefit to humanity.

And,

> The government of the Republic of China considers that the restoration of freedom to its people on the mainland is its sacred mission. It believes that the foundation of this mission resides in the minds and the hearts of the Chinese people and that the principal means of successfully achieving its mission is the implementation of Dr. Sun Yat-sen's three people's principles (nationalism, democracy and social well-being) and not the use of force.

These declarations have significance not just for China but for all the Far East and indeed for all the free world. They give welcome reassurances that the Republic of China will not by any rash act engulf the world in war. Also they assure that Chinese culture will live on as a symbol and inspiration to all the Chinese people and indeed to all of us.

A Noble Strategy of Victory

There are some who question whether the foreign policies we are following will succeed.

It can be affirmed with absolute confidence that our policies will succeed if they are steadfastly pursued.

Materialistic despotisms, with their iron discipline, their mechanistic performance, their hard and shiny exterior, always seem formidable. Democracies seem to stumble and falter; they advertise their differences and always seem vulnerable. But history has demonstrated again and again that democracies are almost always stronger than they seem and despotisms are always more vulnerable than they appear. For example: It is impossible for Communist nations to develop into modern industrial states without a large degree of education. But minds so educated also penetrate the fallacies of Marxism and increasingly resist conformity.

Also there are increasing demands on the part of the subject peoples for more consumer goods, for more of the fruits of their labor. These demands cannot be indefinitely repressed or satisfied merely with recurrent promises.

Such internal pressures are bound to alter the character of the Communist regimes, particularly if these regimes are denied the glamor and prestige of great external successes.

It may be recalled that when Khrushchev, in 1956, attacked the abuses of Stalin he explained that they could not have been corrected earlier because "many victories were gained during his lifetime."

To deny external successes to international communism is not merely a negative, defensive policy. It accelerates the evolution within the Sino-Soviet bloc of governmental policies which will increasingly seek the welfare of their own peoples rather than exploit these peoples in the interest of world conquest.

If the non-Communist nations hold fast to policies which deter armed aggression, if they prevent subversion through economic and revolutionary processes, and, above all, if they demonstrate the good fruits of freedom, then we can know that freedom will prevail.

President Eisenhower, speaking in Paris at the NATO meeting a year ago, outlined the policies of the free world. Concluding, he said, "There lies before the free nations a clear possibility of peaceful triumph. There is a noble strategy of victory—not victory over any peoples but victory for all peoples."

That is the strategy to which we are dedicated. Its price will be high, not only in terms of money but above all in terms of will, of perseverance, of faith. Given those qualities, victory is assured.

BANNING NUCLEAR TESTS [7]

HUBERT H. HUMPHREY, JR.[8]

Senator Hubert H. Humphrey, Jr., of Minnesota gave this address before the United States Senate on January 20, 1959, on the problem of banning nuclear tests in view of new scientific data on the detection of underground explosions.

At this time negotiations between the United States, the United Kingdom, and the Soviet Union were under way at Geneva, Switzerland, for the purpose of drafting a treaty on the discontinuance of nuclear weapons tests, "under effective inspection and safeguards." Agreement had been reached on four articles of a proposed treaty. Senator Humphrey as Senate chairman of the Disarmament Subcommittee had served as one of the congressional advisers at the negotiations.

Behind the negotiations had been the fact that scientists from the United States and other Western nations had reached agreement with scientists from the Soviet bloc at a technical conference during the summer of 1958 on ways to detect violations. On January 5, 1959, however, the White House issued a statement to the effect that new scientific data have appeared which indicate that it would be difficult to distinguish underground explosions from earthquakes.

Senator Humphrey in his speech analyzed at length the significance of the new hindrance and proposed research to refine methods of recognizing earthquakes as distinguished from nuclear firings. He emphasized that "it is important that our negotiators should proceed to try to negotiate a treaty. We must not . . . conclude that it will not be possible to have an effective system to monitor an agreement to suspend nuclear weapons tests."

Senator Humphrey had stirred wide interest throughout America in his report of his eight-hour personal interview with Premier Khrushchev in Moscow on December 1, 1958. In the political campaign of 1958 Humphrey had been a vigorous Democratic debater. His sentiments and philosophy were decidedly progressive; and his voice, bodily action, dynamic personality and extempore skill all contributed to his platform persuasiveness. He continued to be prominently mentioned as a possible nominee of his party for the presidency in 1960.

[7] From the *Congressional Record.* 105:862-867 (daily edition). January 20, 1959. The length of this address permits only a concluding section to be reprinted here.

[8] For biographical note, see Appendix.

In our effort to set up an effective control system we must make whatever improvements are deemed feasible and warranted. The conference of experts agreed to provide that the international control organization should put into effect a scientific research program, with the aim of raising the scientific standard of the system. For example, there should be consideration given to a proposal to have nuclear tests—of equal number from the United States, United Kingdom, and the U.S.S.R.—undertaken under international control for the purpose of furthering research and knowledge in this field.

I discussed this matter at considerable length with the political leaders in the Soviet Union. I also discussed the matter of nuclear tests with the Deputy Foreign Minister of the Soviet Union, Mr. Kuznetsov, who was the spokesman for the Soviet Union in the Surprise Attack Conference in Geneva. I felt it was important that there be some firsthand discussion of the matter for purposes of information.

What Are the Risks?

Let us also keep in mind that the risks we are taking if we sign a treaty to discontinue nuclear tests do not threaten our actual survival. Are we giving up all our bombs—nuclear as well as conventional? No, not one will be lost. Are we giving up our missiles, or even our testing of missiles, in this proposed agreement? No, we can keep what few we have, and unless another agreement is negotiated we and the Soviets can keep on producing and developing as many missiles as money, brains, and energy permit. I suggest we get busy.

We can still keep producing all the nuclear weapons our tests and research have thus far developed. So really we are not engaged in a risk which entails our survival.

The risk in this agreement is that we would curtail our development of nuclear weapons insofar as further tests are necessary to develop improved designs. There is also the risk that the Russians will cheat and will not get caught. Our government claims that we now are ahead of them, both in nuclear weapons production and in the number of tests held to date.

If the Russians did cheat, how many tests might they conduct, and would they all go undetected? Even with very small tests where the probability of detection might be small, the possibility of a violator being detected would increase with the number of tests conducted. Given the right of inspection, are the Russians so clever and are we so stupid that they would not be caught?

Warning to the Soviets

In encouraging and urging our negotiators to continue to try to negotiate a test ban, I believe the Soviets should be dealt with firmly. They must know that there are two conditions for a test ban treaty that must be present. I have made it quite clear in my conversations with the Soviets that these conditions are imperative. One is that there must be no veto by them, by us, or anyone else, which prevents an investigation of the source of a suspicious signal. The right of effective inspection must be preserved. We should be prepared to submit to this. And so should they. The Russians keep calling for equality. Well, on this we should be prepared to have equal treatment: no veto for us; no veto for them. If they do not accept this principle, then the negotiations cannot be fruitful.

The second condition is that there must be some way to improve the control system as flaws in it are observed. The results of our recent underground tests probably are indicative of the amount and type of information that can be learned about the interior of the earth and the effects and characteristics of manmade explosions as well as earthquakes.

I may add that the methodology which is required for high altitude explosions also needs to be further improved and explored. High altitude explosions need a most careful type of detection system. It seems as though many improvements will be needed. I would even think that some modifications of the system created by the scientists last summer might be undertaken. If the Russians refuse to look facts in the face, if they refuse to consider any of the ways to improve the control system, then this is an indication that they will reject any improvements in the future. If this is their attitude we should know it now.

These views I have expressed to the Russian negotiators when I was in Geneva last fall. I have expressed them unqualifiedly also to Premier Khrushchev. I said to them, and I repeat now, that any agreement which lends itself to evasion will only increase tension and provoke hostility. It is my view that no agreement is preferable to one that would be ineffective.

I also said that the world has a right to expect the nuclear powers to come to an agreement which is sound and enforceable. Such an agreement can be arrived at.

What Are the Possible Gains?

In conclusion, I want to stress that we must look at the advantages of a controlled suspension of nuclear tests in addition to assessing the risks. If a test ban agreement is reached it will be the first break in the arms race since it began several years ago. It could pave the way to further progress in reducing and controlling the weapons of war. This surely is needed. I believe it would help reduce the terrible tension that now exists between the free world and the Soviet bloc. It may make possible a more rational discussion and negotiation of other problems which divide the world into hostile camps. It would be a major political breakthrough, a major change in the concept of an Iron Curtain that is drawn between us and the Soviet people.

If the negotiations are to fail, then it must be the intransigence of the Soviets which is the cause. Failure must not be charged to us. We must continue to negotiate to see if an agreement can be reached.

Mr. President, the world is concerned about this arms race. While it is imperative, so long as the race continues, that we be strong, united, and prepared, I think it is equally important that the best talent of our country be dedicated to finding a just and an enduring peace.

I sometimes wonder if we really devote as much time to finding ways to peace as we do to finding ways to the moon and to outer space. I think it would be a good question sometimes to ask ourselves how much time, money, energy, and sacrifice we devote to finding ways to a just and enduring peace as compared to the time, money, energy, skill, and resources which we devote to the terrible weapons which threaten the life of God's creation, that we put into, even, the exploration of outer space.

I have said before that I think the real problem in the world is not outer space; it is inner man. The sooner we do something about man and man's relationship to his fellow men, the sooner we shall be able to do much more about man's relationship to outer space.

WESTERN EUROPEAN ATTITUDES, AUGUST 1958 [9]

ERIC SEVAREID [10]

Eric Sevareid broadcast to the United States and the world this talk from Paris on August 29, 1958, at the end of his summer "vacation." It was one of the regular newscasts delivered by him over the Columbia Broadcasting System.

In August twenty years earlier Sevareid began his career as news analyst and reporter for CBS. He followed the French army and air force in France and in Belgium; reported the surrender of French armies; later broadcast from England, France, Holland, and other European zones, and from various Latin American countries. His interpretation of French and European sentiments during July and August 1958 thus reflected his long background as student, journalist, and radio commentator in Europe.

As chief Washington correspondent for CBS in 1958, he delivered nightly radio commentaries on people and events that were uniformly penetrating and provocative. He helped make the observance of National Radio Month meaningful.

Sevareid has spoken out with clarity, calm reasoning, and over-all grasp of current political-social-economic problems. His oral style is original and brisk; his delivery is positive and well paced; and his personality is a favorable factor in his television panel participation, as well as on radio.

Sevareid's *Not So Wild a Dream* (1946) presents an autobiographical report of the early home, school, and college training and experiences that largely account for his methods and attitudes as journalist and broadcaster.

Good evening. This is the end of a two months' sojourn in Europe for this reporter, who normally looks at the world of man's affairs through the lens of Washington. There is something restorative of the spirit, in any change from the routine and the accustomed; but there is something about Europe in these days that is especially comforting, it seems to me. In America there is a sense of power and forward motion and from there one often thinks of Western Europe as a troubled and decaying society, forever on a financial or other brink.

[9] Text furnished by Eric Sevareid, with permission for this reprint.

[10] For biographical note, see Appendix.

There is no doubt that in terms of relative power and importance Europe has declined in our times; Germany remains divided; Britain has lost much of her great empire, Italy all of hers and France is irrevocably losing hers.

But the resources of man are endlessly underestimated; and as this process of decline in power goes on, European life itself grows steadily better and brighter; everywhere here, while the nation declines, the individual, it seems to me, advances his lot and grows in consequence; for most people here life is good; and those who get the short shrift in the benefits of this munificent age are acutely aware of that, and slowly they rectify the balance.

The words of Mr. Khrushchev to Mr. Stevenson, that the world inevitably moves toward communism—these words make strange reading here in Western Europe. Never before, to me, have these societies seemed further away from Marxism; in this time of surprising plenty, hardly a Socialist party from Norway on down any longer struggles for the reconstruction of society—merely for its amelioration.

Perhaps, in the sunlit charm of these ancient cities which have survived all the trials of history, one's sense of danger is lulled away. Yet it must be said that Washington's view of world affairs—that crisis sense, that feeling of a race with Russia for this gadget or that area lest all be lost—it must be said that this view of the present world is quite alien to most Europeans as far as a visitor may judge. Individually, Europeans may not believe very much in happiness as the conscious good; but they do believe in the continuity of life; they have suffered—and survived—so much for two thousand years that the imagined picture of civilization's Armageddon does not come easily to their minds. If my antenna is sensitive at all, there is extremely little belief here that Russia either wants war or will be at war with the rest of us, short of accident or leadership gone mad.

And this leads one toward the heart of the European uneasiness about American foreign policy; Europeans dearly wish that we would relax, not only in our frenetic personal lives at home, but in our life as a nation within the mutual world; they are a little impatient with the exigencies of our domestic politics, and therefore, in every country, you find leaders despairing of our policy toward Eastern Europe and toward China. Rightly, or very wrongly, they would accept the status of East Europe and of China and proceed on that basis; beyond that, the thoughtful among them, I believe, give grateful welcome to America's new role on the whole world scene and know, in their hearts, its selfless nature.

The anti-Americanism of cafe society and the literary salons over here is not something to lose sleep about; it does not go very deep among the ordinary people. Those little State Department booklets issued to traveling Americans, advising on their behavior abroad, are not only insulting, but quite unneeded. For, and it is borne upon one even more strongly by travel, there is among Americans collectively a great goodness, and among them individually a natural warmth, and these are among the steadier things in this unsteady world.

This is Eric Sevareid in Paris.

AT THE BRUSSELS EXPOSITION [11]

HERBERT HOOVER [12]

Former President Herbert Hoover gave this Independence Day address at the Brussels Exposition, on July 4, 1958. Appointed special envoy of the United States by President Eisenhower, Mr. Hoover interpreted to the people of the world who were visiting the fair the true picture of the American dream of freedom, independence, and self-determination. A month away from his eighty-fourth birthday, he delivered an address that will stand as one of the best of his long and distinguished public career. In language, sentiment, and appeal it ranks with the important documents of American public address. The speaker despite his age continued to speak with firmness, clarity, and alertness to his immediate audience. Said Senator Alexander Smith of New Jersey in the Senate on July 7, "Mr. President, the visit of former President Hoover to Belgium over the Fourth of July weekend has filled the news with statements of gratitude of the Belgian people to a great American."

On July 5 the former President addressed the Belgian people. This speech, extempore and highly reminiscent, more moving in its personal elements and originality than the address of the preceding day, ended with these eloquent words: "The greatness of a nation does not lie in the numbers of its people, nor in their economic and industrial accomplishments. It lies in the spiritual and moral foundations of its people. Perhaps as few other men, I know the indomitable spirit, the courage, and the character of the Belgian nation and the glorious record of its long past." [13]

It is a high honor for me to come here as the special envoy of President Eisenhower. He extends his greetings and congratulations and those of the American people to the King and people of Belgium for this great Exposition.

This visit also gives me the opportunity to refresh my friendship with the Belgian people, which has now lasted for more than forty-four years. Tomorrow I have the privilege of speaking especially to my friends in Belgium.

[11] Text provided by former President Herbert Hoover with permission for this reprint. For text see also *Congressional Record*. 104:11823-5 (daily edition). July 7, 1958.

[12] For biographical note, see Appendix.

[13] For further comment on Herbert Hoover as a speaker, see the Cumulative Author Index for references to his speeches in earlier volumes.

Belgium has organized at this fair a magnificent portrayal of her own achievements and those of many nations. By this great exposition, she may contribute to lessening the tensions which haunt the world.

The Invisible Forces Radiating from Nations

But magnificent as these exhibits are, they cannot in the larger sense visibly portray the invisible forces of governmental, economic, moral, and spiritual values in the daily life of a nation. Nor can exhibits alone show the spread of these invisible forces beyond their frontiers.

Mine has been a long life. In that time I have lived and worked among more than fifty nations. I have not visited them as a tourist; I have had some part in the lives of their peoples. And I can claim some understanding of their problems, their ideals, and their aspirations.

In these troubled times no one can ignore the crises which beset the world. But here at this fair, in this climate of friendly competition, criticism of other nations would be entirely out of place.

It is, however, fitting that the representative of a particular nation should interpret here the ideals, the aspirations, and the way of life of his own people. Such discussion adds to this exposition's panorama of mankind's progress.

I am informed that I am speaking tonight over the radio and through the press to many nations.

And in so doing, I remind you that we Americans are descended from every nation in Europe. Therefore, you have some responsibility for these invisible forces radiating from my country.

I would be proud if on this occasion, I could contribute a mite to the better understanding of my people. And I would be especially happy if I could help the thinking of the oncoming youth in the world, who are today groping for light as to the future.

These subjects are the more appropriate for me on this day which has been set aside by the exposition to honor the Independence Day of the United States.

Invisible Forces from American Independence

It was on this day, 182 years ago, that our Founding Fathers consecrated a new republic "under the protection of Divine Providence." They dedicated it as a stronghold for the dignity of the individual and his rights to religious, economic, social, and political liberty under the rule of law.

But the ideals in a nation do not spring alone from their method of government. They spring also from the depths of their religious faith, from their pride in country, from their trials, from their glories of victory, and from their memories of their great leaders.

No American is so silly as to claim that the rights of man to freedom were discovered in the United States on July 4, 1776.

Since the dawn of history there has existed in the minds of men the longing and the hope for national independence and for individual freedom. That spark has many times broken through oppression and burst into victorious flame. Tragically, it has been crushed not once but many times, and its flame has often become ashes. But never has the iron foot of oppression been potent enough to stamp out the living spark in the ashes.

That spark again sprang to flame in the New World—never since to be extinguished. It became once more a flame that lighted the skies and all the earth.

Enduring Government in Free People

One of the interpretations of my country concerns the method of free government. For governments of free men are confronted with many problems. One of them is enduring protection of the rights and liberties of men from destructive internal forces which they themselves create. During the last century, new and revolutionary discoveries in science, great inventions, and the changes in social thought have brought many problems to free governments.

I do not need to recall that we have two major methods of government among free peoples. The United States adopted a method where the executive is separated from the legislative powers, and the election of the individual executive and legislative officials is for fixed terms.

The British hold to the parliamentary method which combines the legislative and administrative powers, and their officials are periodically subject to election—all at the same time. That method has operated admirably where its base rests upon a majority political party.

But, especially since the First World War, the host of internal problems confronting parliamentary government on the European continent has resulted in the development of a multitude of factional political parties. Their inability to reach determined and constructive solutions of their national problems has brought a strangling chaos in government. Since the First World War fifteen European nations, in despair, have turned to dictatorships. And it has been my fate to witness on the ground the forces which led to their collapse.

The American method is not perfect, but for 182 years it has sustained stability in our country through every crisis and, in the main, brought an orderly progress in the midst of new inventions and ideas.

Perhaps our experience in the separation of executive and legislative powers and the election of officials for fixed terms has uses for other free men.

The World Service of American Productivity

I have little reason to elaborate here upon the success of our system of regulated economic freedom. It has built-in impulses of initiative, energy, ambition, and opportunity. It has brought stupendous benefits to the American people.

But to relate the huge benefits my people have received is not my purpose here. The world's interest is that our productivity has created great margins which have enabled us to support the freedom of mankind, and to help lift the world's burdens of disaster and poverty.

At my time of life and because of my experience in many nations, I know that far more vital than even economic blessings are the spiritual and moral impulses and ideals which motivate the lives of peoples.

Compassion

In interpreting the ideals of my country, I must include the spirit of compassion towards suffering humanity. It spreads from every American home to all mankind. I need only to recall the great famines which have inevitably followed these two score years of world wars. The American people with other nations met these emergencies. But the United States carried the major burden. By longer hours of labor they stimulated production. They denied themselves food and clothing that more than one billion of peoples all over the world might have the margins on which to live and to hope for a better day.

This spirit of compassion has contributed also to the rehabilitation of many millions of children, diseased and debilitated by famine. Thereby, the world has been saved from the political and moral dangers of millions of distorted bodies and distorted minds. And this compassion has also been extended to Communist Russia.

Sharing Scientific Discovery and Invention

One of the several tests of a nation's contributions to mankind is its scientific discoveries and the application of these discoveries to all human comfort and progress.

I could recite a long list of such discoveries and inventions that my countrymen have contributed to the world.

And my country in turn has benefited by the application of the great scientific discoveries and inventions of many other nations.

But I am not as much concerned with which nation discovered or invented what, as I am with wider distribution of each nation's discoveries and inventions over the world. Thereby sweat is taken from the brows of men and women. Their hours of labor are reduced. Their days of leisure are increased. Their opportunities for recreation and participation in the arts and intellectual life are expanded. And above all, scientific discovery lifts the burden of poverty everywhere.

No longer do these discoveries come only from a solitary scientist or inventor. They are now more often the product of teamwork by many skilled scientists and engineers.

There is now some cooperation in organization of world-wide research. It is an aspiration of my country to see such cooperation expanded. Thus the march of progress in the world would be faster.

The Atom—and Peace

There is one scientific discovery which deeply concerns every human being. The theoretical deductions of European scientists as to the constitution of the atom were harnessed in America into a gigantic source of power.

I have no need to say that it can bring benefits to mankind, and it can be used to destroy civilization.

My countrymen pray daily alongside hundreds of millions of other peace-loving people that there should be a real disarmament, which will include disarming the atom.

The Need to Correct Some Misrepresentations

There can be no interpretation of the American way of life in its effect upon other nations without reference to the false legends, misrepresentations, and vicious propaganda which haunt the free world.

We are often depicted as living under the control of wicked men who exploit our economic life through gigantic trusts and huge corporations. They are supposed to grind the faces of the poor and to exploit other nations. All this ignores the fact that our laws for nearly seventy years have prohibited the existence of trusts and cartels. In few other nations have the fundamentals of fair and open competition been so zealously maintained.

This competition has spurred our industries to adopt every labor-saving device. And to create them, there are more than five thousand industrial research laboratories that pour out new ideas which become open to all the world.

Insofar as large corporations are concerned, they are the property of millions of our people. The largest of them has more than 1.5 million individual stockholders, not one of whom owns more than one thirtieth of one per cent of the corporation.

Another example of this propaganda is that we are infested with gigantic individual fortunes which dominate the life of our people.

Any regulated free economic system permits men of exceptional ability or luck to accumulate great property. We have had a few hundred such accumulations. But our graduated taxes rise to 90 per cent of their yearly incomes. And up to 77 per cent of their estates are taken by taxes when the owner passes on. Thus, most of these accumulations tend to fade away.

But these large fortunes have been of profound importance to other nations. From them have come many of our great educational and scientific institutions, whose beneficent work has been extended to all the peoples of the world. One of these institutions, through organized research and its world-wide applications, practically eliminated yellow fever from the whole earth.

There Is No American Imperialism

Probably the greatest misrepresentation of our ideals is that we are imperialistically-minded and that we daily practice imperialism. It would seem that the world might take account of the Monroe Doctrine, whereby we have aided our Latin American neighbors to secure their freedoms. I could also recall our giving freedom to Cuba and the Philippines and our urging of independence for Puerto Rico.

Moreover, in the last forty years, invariably at the request of nations struggling against oppression or military aggression, our sons have fought and died in three great wars. They died that more freedom would come to mankind and that the world might have a lasting peace.

Never after victory did we ask for an acre of territory, except a few military bases to protect the free nations. We have never asked for reparations or economic privileges. On the contrary, we made gigantic gifts and loans to aid nations in their defense and reconstruction, including Communist Russia.

When it was evident that nations could not repay these loans, we made no demands for repayment.

Our people have willingly borne back-breaking taxes in these efforts without any hope of returns. And they are today continuing this huge burden of taxation to aid in protecting the freedom of mankind and to relieve peoples from poverty.

I would not have believed in the face of this world-wide record that peoples with a free press could be imposed upon by such propaganda.

There is no imperialism in either our hearts or in our government.

Nor Aggression

This record of the past century should also prove there is no military aggression in the American mind or heart. Truly, we maintain an enormous military force. But it is maintained solely as a deterrent to attack upon free nations.

A Caution

It is my hope that this interpretation of my country may aid our friends in free countries to answer this propaganda.

And I would not be your friend if I did not speak frankly now.

These misrepresentations and this propaganda are inciting physical attacks upon American citizens, upon our officials, and abuse of our country. They discourage the American people and increase opposition to cooperation with other nations in maintaining defense and in aiding relief from poverty and disaster.

Forty years ago such attitudes contributed to the retreat of the American people behind a barbed-wire entanglement around the Western Hemisphere. I have little fear of such a retreat today. But the danger signal is up.

America Has No Wish to Impose Its Way of Life

At this point I may inject another interpretation of the American people. We have no desire to impose our formula of life or method of government upon other nations. We make no claim that our system or our people are perfect. As human beings are not usually perfect, we share the domestic imperfections of all free peoples.

And my countrymen are in constant motion to eradicate our failings—and when I am home I have often joined them. But the purpose of this address is not our domestic troubles but the better understanding of our ideals and aspirations which radiate to other nations.

In Conclusion

At the beginning of this address I stated that I would be especially happy if I could help the thinking of the oncoming youth in the world who are today groping for light as to the future.

Therefore, I wish to conclude this evening by speaking directly to you of the new generation. I recall to you that a great American President pointed out that to assure the progress of civilization and lasting peace, the world must be made "safe for democracy." But the word "democracy" has been so corrupted that I would prefer to say to you:

"We must unceasingly strive by all peaceable means to make the world safe for representative government."

From representative government alone can come respect for your dignity as men and women, your flowering as individuals, your right to a rising chance in life, to self-expression, and to security from sodden uniformity.

May God bless you all.

INDUSTRY AND LABOR

PRICE AND THE PUBLIC INTEREST [1]

Roger M. Blough [2]

Roger Blough, chairman of the board of the United States Steel Corporation, gave this address before the Economic Club of Detroit on September 15, 1958.

The issues which he pointedly discussed after his whimsical opening had to do with four major questions: (1) Are those responsible for the "campaign of misinterpretation" of industry's policies aiming to establish a "profitless profit system"? (2) Are they supporting a drive for peacetime price controls? (3) Are they throwing up a smoke screen about the role that Congress has played in this problem of inflation? (4) Are their interests and methods genuinely in the public interest?

The object of the campaign, he argued, was to blame industry for inflation. His analysis and considerable evidence pointed to other causes. He predicted that a profitless profit system would result if wage increases continued. He placed the blame for inflation on heavy Federal spending, the growing Federal deficit, and the wave of union-sparked wage increases. These wages, he contended, are a major cause of the rising cost of living. Industry's dwindling profits and rising costs, he concluded, are weakening the United States in the economic struggle with Russia.

Blough, a graduate of the Yale Law School, practiced law before New York and Pennsylvania courts and the United States Supreme Court, and served as the United States Steel Corporation's general solicitor. (The speech printed below is in form a legal plea.) He has an excellent voice, ease of manner before his business-economic audiences. He is a worthy successor to the former president of U.S. Steel, Benjamin F. Fairless.

Up to now, I have enjoyed your hospitality very much. It is always a pleasure to visit this great city of industrial achievement, and I appreciate especially the opportunity to congratulate the Economic Club of Detroit as it opens the twenty-fifth year of its distinguished history.

[1] Text furnished by Philip H. Adams, vice president (public relations) of the United States Steel Corporation, and reprinted here through the courtesy of Roger M. Blough.

[2] For biographical note, see Appendix.

But according to the literature which Mr. Crow [Allen Benjamin Crow, president of the club] was good enough to send me a few weeks ago, I find that 902 speakers have preceded me to this rostrum and have discussed 817 different subjects. Furthermore, I note that, almost without exception, these speakers had attained national or international renown as authorities on the topics of their choice. Add to this the fact that several of these gentlemen were outstanding representatives of the steel industry, and you can judge for yourselves how remote is the prospect that number 903 on your list can say anything on any subject that hasn't already been better said by the other 902.

If there is any faint hope for me at all, under these distressing circumstances, it lies in the unhappy fact that, in recent years, I have had certain regrettable experiences with steel prices, and thus have acquired a sufficient number of wounds and bruises to qualify me as something of an authority on How Not to Win Friends and Influence People—especially in Washington.

Now I recognize, of course, that many of you in this audience are important customers of ours . . . and when I say *important* customers—believe me, gentlemen, we have no other kind. So this is not, perhaps, the most appropriate place in which to discuss the recent price increase. In fact, it occurs to me that Daniel's situation in the lion's den was hardly more precarious than mine. I console myself, however, with the comforting thought that—unlike the lions—you customers have already enjoyed a full meal.

Nevertheless, perhaps I'd better begin by saying to you gentlemen, very simply and very sincerely, that I would like never to see another price go up!

Like all of you here—and like every other businessman in America—I am deeply disturbed by the steady postwar upsurge in the prices of both goods and services. I am even more disturbed by the persistent inflation that has caused those prices to rise. I am equally disturbed by the headlong increase in wage costs which has contributed so importantly to the inflationary spiral. I am further disturbed by the skyrocketing price of government and by the consequent Federal deficit which is a major source of this inflation. But most of all, I am disturbed by what appears to be a conscious or unconscious campaign of misinterpretation and even misrepresentation, the purpose of which is to place all blame for the inflation upon the pricing policies of American industry. In fact, "disturbed" is an inadequate word to describe my reaction to what frequently amounts to a campaign of calumny peddled from high places by those who pose as defenders of the public interest.

Thus far, these mistaken champions of the public interest have concentrated their attack primarily upon three industries—steel, automobiles and oil; but, if pursued, the natural result of this campaign will be to inflame public opinion against business generally and eventually to lay the groundwork for someone seizing an ever-larger measure of control over its affairs.

So I would like, today, to talk with you for a little while about this matter of Price and the Public Interest—to examine with you some of the aspects of this propaganda campaign as it has been applied to steel, and to discover, if we can, whose public interest our attackers are serving.

Now the theme song of the campaigners, of course, is that a rise in the price of steel is little less than a national calamity. It makes no difference how small the price increase may be, nor how inadequate it is in the face of the ballooning costs of both wages and materials. *Any* price increase of *any* size is immediately denounced as unjustified. The campaigners proclaim that it will touch off another disastrous round of inflation and that it will cause consumers to "sit on their hands" and thus plunge the nation back into the recession from which it is just now emerging. In short, they chorus that rising steel prices are the cause of inflation, recession, and all other economic ills.

And this—to put it as politely as I can—is a fairy tale. You might even say that it is a Grimm fairy tale. Let's look into it a bit.

Last year, in preparing to launch its attack upon the steel industry, the antimonopoly subcommittee of the United States Senate carefully picked a number of economists to come before it and show how the so-called "administered prices" of business had caused inflation. The experiment was not an unqualified success from the committee's point of view.

Several of the economists pointed an accusing finger at "administered wages" and other rising costs; and one of the group —Professor Richard Ruggles of Yale—presented an exhaustive study of the government's cost of living index which revealed this challenging fact: That since 1951, the price of products—or things—had risen only 2 per cent, while the price of services —or non-things, such as transportation, medical care, laundry, haircuts, rent and so on—had risen 21 per cent. In other words, the rise in the price of all the manufactured articles and other things that people bought had been negligible. And having presented this evidence, Dr. Ruggles concluded with these significant words—and I quote them exactly from the record. He said:

> It is not possible to maintain, in view of the statistical evidence, that administered prices have been primarily responsible for the inflationary spiral.

Now it may surprise you to learn that—through some mystifying oversight of its staff, no doubt—the majority report of the committee fails even to mention Dr. Ruggles' testimony. Perhaps the committee majority felt that the facts he presented were not in the public interest.

Also in the same committee record are facts from a similar study which was published in the New York *Times* last year. They show that while the price of steel had increased 14 per cent since 1951, the price of household appliances, such as washing machines and the like, had actually declined by 13 per cent during the same period. And in this connection the *Times* made a statement that is at once so true and so astonishing, that again I want to quote it verbatim. Said the *Times*:

> Though it may seem surprising, the price of steel could practically double and the cost of living would hardly show it!

—And gentlemen, do you know that by the strangest of coincidences, that evidence is nowhere mentioned in the majority report of the committee either?

But even more puzzling to me, is what I might call the strange case of the forgotten price reduction.

Some of you may recall that just ten years ago this summer—in what was then hailed as an outstanding act of industrial statesmanship in a period of serious inflation—United States Steel refused a wage increase to its workers and reduced the price of steel by amounts ranging up to $5 a ton on those products which might be expected to produce the most immediate effect upon the consumer's pocketbook and the cost of living.

At that time the cost of living was rising at a frightening rate—fully four times as fast, in fact, as it has during the past year; and do you remember what happened to it after the price cut?

Well, it went up still faster. The march of inflation was not even fazed by the steel price reduction. It moved on, unabated; and within a few months, U. S. Steel had to raise wages, rescind the reduction and increase its prices in a belated effort to catch up with the tail end of the wage-cost procession that had already passed it by.

And then an interesting thing happened. No sooner had steel prices been *raised* than the cost of living began to drop. Month after month it went down until it reach the lowest level in twenty-two months! So here was a kind of laboratory test, if you will, which disproved completely the fairy tales that the campaigners keep telling. The whole story—fully documented—was presented in evidence to the Senate committee, and the senior senator from Tennessee, as chairman of the group, was present and heard the entire testimony regarding this price reduction.

Yet the *Congressional Record* shows that only six weeks ago—on July 30, to be exact—a member of the committee rose on the floor of the Senate and said:

> I should like to ask one more question of the distinguished Senator from Tennesseee. Does he remember any testimony that the steel companies have ever reduced their prices?

To which Senator Kefauver replied:

> I do not remember any!

Now I would not want to overemphasize this lapse of memory nor to examine too closely its relationship to the public interest. I would merely point out that certainly it served the interests of those who would confuse the American people into believing that there is an immediate and inseparable cause and effect connection between steel prices and the cost of living—that a steel price increase is the cause and a rise in the cost of living is invariably the effect.

No; the campaigners go merrily along, dinning their theme song into our tired ears. They tell us that the higher cost of steel will raise the price of everything from tractors to hairpins; that it will boost the price of everything from automobiles to safety pins; and they express concern about the price of appliances and bobby pins.

Now this universal preoccupation with the price of pins embraces an emotional appeal that is sure-fire stuff. You know the ancient tale. "For the want of a nail, the shoe was lost." And what could be lost for the want of a safety pin is almost too horrendous to contemplate.

But be of good cheer, gentlemen. The nation is not yet undone! I am happy to inform you that—according to the government's wholesale price index—the price of fasteners—including safety pins, hairpins, bobby pins and zippers—has *declined* more than 14 per cent in the past ten years!

So let's face up to the facts.

And the fact is that in making all of the millions of products that they turn out, American manufacturers use many thousands of kinds of different materials, one of which is steel. The fact also is that when the price of any of these materials goes up, the manufacturer's costs go up accordingly; and that somehow under our competitive system he must meet these higher costs or go broke. The fact is further that American manufacturers have done a magnificent job of offsetting much of this higher cost through research, improved technology and the investment of vast sums of money in new, more efficient tools of production. So instead of being pyramided and passed along to the consumer—as the campaigners tell us they are—these costs have been absorbed in large measure.

But the most important fact, of course, is that the intrinsic or basic cost of the materials that go into all of the products that are made in America is only a small percentage of the total cost of those products.

Commenting on the price of steel, the other day, an official of the Ford Motor Company was quoted as saying:

> Labor costs mean more to the auto industry than material costs. About 80 per cent of what you pay for a car goes for labor and only about 20 per cent for materials—including steel.

And that, of course, is not only true of automobiles, it is true throughout industry generally.

If you took all of the products that are made in America, put them in one huge pile, and added up the price tags on the lot, upwards of three quarters of this total value would represent the employment costs that were incurred all along the line of production. The remaining quarter or less would cover not only the basic cost of all the raw materials, but would also pay for the rental of property, the interest on debt, and the dividends that pay for use of all of the tools of production that were employed in the manufacture of those products.

So the truth of the matter is that the effect of a rise in the price of steel—or of any other material—is so insignificant in comparison to the overwhelming importance of a rise in wage costs, that it is not—and never can be—a controlling, or even a dominant factor in the price of finished articles.

And this, of course, is precisely the fact that certain members of the Senate antimonopoly subcommittee have been trying so successfully to ignore.

When the steel companies—after a costly five-week strike—reluctantly signed their present labor agreement with the union, two years ago, everyone knew that the annual boosts in employment costs provided in that contract could not possibly be absorbed through an improvement in what some people call productivity, and could therefore only be met by a rise in prices. There was no secret about that. You knew it; we knew it; the union knew it; the public knew it; and the Government knew it. But the very same senators who are now crying havoc at the rise in steel prices were strangely silent then. Did any one of them ever raise his voice against these inflationary wage demands? Did any one of them even faintly suggest that such wage demands might not be entirely in the public interest?

No; there wasn't so much as a whisper from them.

Ever since last spring, the automobile companies here in Detroit have been fighting to hold the wage-price line, knowing what the effect of the union's wage demands would be on the price of the 1959 models. But they have been fighting alone while the Senate subcommittee looks with studied care in some other direction.

So here we find an interesting study in practical politics. The committee majority professes to be amazed by the fact that industrial prices have risen at a time when demand was falling off in the market place. This, they say, is in defiance of all of the natural laws of economics; and they try to conjure up evidence to show that big, bad business monopoly has caused this unusual phenomenon.

Yet with astonishing success, they have diligently failed to recognize a truly unique economic phenomenon which clearly accounts for the first: the fact that wage costs have never stopped their upward push, even though there are 5 million unemployed. Could it possibly be that this strange, and economically inexplicable behavior of wage rates has had, in baseball language, an assist from the massive power over costs—and therefore prices—which Congress itself has conferred upon the great national unions?

I merely ask.

Gentlemen, this subcommittee has spent hundreds of thousands of dollars of Federal funds to investigate prices in some of our major industries; and I am sure that the companies which have been haled before it have, together, spent many times that sum in preparing and presenting every fact and figure about their business that could be meaningful and legitimately helpful to the committee.

Had the committee used this material in a real, unbiased, scholarly and nonpolitical effort to enlist the American people in an all-out attack upon inflation at its actual sources, every penny of this money would have been well spent, and the investigation would have performed a great service to the nation.

But the committee majority has chosen instead an opposite course, some of the reasons for which we can only surmise.

This political world being what it is, it could hardly be expected that the members of the committee majority could find the time or the inclination to point out that a basic source of the present inflation lies in the fiscal action of a Congress which, in two years, has raised the *price of government* by $10 billion, and has left behind it a $12 billion deficit—an action which is certain to give inflation an added boost.

Neither, I suspect, would it be in the personal political interest of the committee majority to expose the extent to which the leadership of labor has been responsible for rising prices.

So the committee majority has chosen to devote its resources to antibusiness attacks on industrial profits—attacks which have already stimulated considerable discussion of peace-time price controls. Let's look at a quick sampling of the kind of misinformation that the taxpayers are getting out of this committee for their money:

The chairman of the committee keeps telling us, twelve months later, that the $6-a-ton price increase of last year has actually cost the direct buyers of steel $540 million and that the cost to the consumer was undoubtedly pyramided to several times that amount.

Passing the fact that there is considerable room for improvement in his level of arithmetical accuracy since the industry shipped just 64,308,000 tons of steel products in the period, the obvious purpose of the chairman is to leave the impression that the dollars from the increased price went into the steel companies' pockets and somehow stayed there. Does he give equal billing to the fact that all the dollars going in went out and more too? And for what? Not for increased dividends, but to pay the increased wages and the other costs incurred during the twelve months that have passed. Proof enough of this is the fact that the industry's profit declined 50 per cent between the first half of last year and the first half of this.

The chairman has also repeatedly stated that most of the wage increase which went into effect last July 1 would be offset by the long-run increase in labor productivity. Now I don't know, of course, just how long a run the Senator has in mind; but the longer we run, at the past rate of wage increases, the worse off we are; for the undisputed evidence in the record of the committee shows that during the past seventeen years, U.S. Steel's employment costs, per man hour, have gone up at an average rate of more than 8 per cent per year, while the government's own reports show that output per man hour in steel has risen by less than 3 per cent per year. And anyone, including the Senator from Tennessee, who can *really* absorb the 8 per cent out of less than 3 per cent, is exactly the man our industry has been looking for, for years!

But the Wonderland arithmetic of the committee reaches its most mystifying proportions when the Senator and some of his colleagues discuss steel profits. They say, for example, that the $6-a-ton price rise of last year was at least twice as much as was necessary to cover the wage increase that became effective at the same time. Beyond that, they insist that the entire cost of the wage increase was offset by a decline in the price of scrap, as if this were all the cost a steel company has; and the conclusions which they draw from these statements are strange and wonderful to behold.

If they were correct, of course—if the increase in wage costs *had* been completely offset by a decline in costs—then, if we may also indulge in the committee majority type of shorthand mathematics—the profits of the steel companies would have gone up by more than $180 million.

The fact is, however, that their profits have *dropped* by $288 million in the twelve months that have passed since that price rise occurred; and the rate of profit has fallen from 7.2 per cent on sales to 6.2 per cent. In other words, had the companies raised the price of steel enough to cover their increased costs and to maintain their former profit rate during this past year of low demand, it would have taken a $10-a-ton price boost, instead of $6, to do the job.

Now the official reports of these companies have been published and are certainly known to the committee and its staff. They show with embarrassing clarity what the facts are; yet these members of the committee continue to repeat such groundless statements. And it makes you wonder whether the committee majority really believes in adequate profits for industry—and whether a business profit is a part of its political philosophy.

Commenting on what he called the "destructive philosophy" of the committee majority, as it would affect any company or industry, Senator Everett Dirksen, in his minority report on the committee's steel hearings, declared:

> Indeed, the majority seems to feel that the attempt of such enterprises to operate profitably on a downward trend in the business cycle is somehow inimical to the national interest.

Further insight into the philosophy which holds that a lack of adequate business profits is somehow in the public interest, was evidenced in the course of a session of the committee a few weeks ago which was devoted exclusively to the excoriation of steel prices and profits. The Senator from Wyoming spoke eloquently of the dangers arising out of the economic cold war which is being waged against us by Soviet Russia, and then said:

> United States Steel, which is in the position of leadership, wants to maintain itself in the black. The Government of the United States is in the red and is going further into the red; and I have no hesitation in saying that unless the leaders of American industry immediately act to help put the United States in the black, instead of letting it drift deeper and deeper into the red, we will not be able successfully to wage this cold war without great losses to industry and to the people alike.

Now I can understand the Senator's deep concern at the progress which Russia has made in the economic cold war against us. I understand it because I share it fully. I can also understand his profound concern over the Federal deficit, for I share that too. But if we are to infer that industry—by making a profit—is causing the Federal Government to "drift deeper and deeper into the red," then his reasoning escapes me.

Consider for a moment that for every dollar of profit corporations make, the Federal Government collects $1.08 in corporate income taxes. The decline in steel profits alone that has occurred in the past year has already cost the Federal Treasury about $300 million; and were steel profits to be wiped out completely, the Treasury would suffer an additional loss of more than $700 million, thus pushing the government just that much farther into the red, enlarging the deficit, and driving our nation closer to the verge of uncontrolled inflation.

Consider, too, that under our Constitution the Senator from Wyoming and his 530 congressional colleagues have the ultimate power to control government expenditures and receipts, and thus they determine what the government's fiscal condition will be. So when the Senator appeals to the leaders of American industry to help put the United States in the black, about the best thing that industry can possibly do to aid the Senator in his dilemma, so far as I can see, is to strive to maintain the profits upon which the government leans so heavily for its revenues.

But above all, consider the nature and the use of corporate profits. What are they?

Well, the fact is that profit, over the years, is nothing more nor less than the price which a corporation must pay for the use of all of the plants, mills, furnaces, machines, tools and other capital assets that it needs in the fabrication of its product. Without sufficient profits, industry can no longer replace its tools of production as fast as they wear out, at which point the workers who once used these tools are without work. Is that in the public interest?

Without adequate profits, industry can no longer adapt the fruits of research and improve—as it constantly has—our nation's standard of living. Is that in the public interest?

Without enough profit, industry can no longer develop the new sources of raw materials that this nation must have. Is that in the public interest?

Neither can industry obtain the new, more efficient machines and techniques that have thus far enabled it to absorb so much of the rising cost of labor and materials. Thus prices will then rise at a headlong pace. Will that be in the public interest?

In short, with American troops maintaining the peace in the Middle East, with the Seventh Fleet alerted at Quemoy, with Russian industrial technology advancing at such a rapid pace as to challenge, seriously, our own, and with the multiple problems of the cold war which so deeply and properly concern the Senator from Wyoming, how can American industry discharge its responsibilities to the national welfare and the national security unless it *does* make a profit large enough to do the enormous job that only a profit can do in the critical years that lie ahead? How else could industry possibly act in the public interest?

Now surely the members of the committee majority, having achieved the high and respected office which they hold, are fully aware of the facts I have presented here today. Why then this dangerous unwillingness to consider those facts, unpalatable as they may be from a short range political point of view? What is the committee majority driving at?

I hope that the answer is not to be found in a statement which was made at a committee meeting last month by the Senator from Wisconsin—but this is what he said:

> "Price control" is a word we always used to be scared of, but we are letting someone else control the price; why can't the American people control the price, through its government?"

I am sorry to say the Senator's statement was warmly endorsed by several members of the committee.

Now it is true that one thing which the responsible public official must constantly guard against is a kind of natural itch to extend the powers of government over everything and everybody. In a way this itch is a sort of occupational hazard endemic in the world of politics, and must always be reckoned with. So it is inevitable, I suppose, that those who are afflicted in this way should try to foist peace-time price and wage controls upon the American people; but surely no responsible member of Congress —knowing that authority and responsibility must go together— would ever seek to do so.

The members of Congress are accountable directly to the people of their respective constituencies. They are not accountable directly to the owners, the customers or the employees of any business or enterprise, as management is. And for government or any committee of Congress to try to usurp the functions of management—either by intimidation or by law—is as alien to our American constitutional concepts as for business to try to usurp the functions of government.

In fact, I can think of nothing that could insure a Soviet victory in the cold war more completely and more quickly than that the self-same members of Congress who have "controlled" the government's finances into the deplorable condition described by the Senator from Wyoming, should now be allowed to "control" American business and industry into a state of acute capital starvation by attempting to regulate all prices, wages and profits from Washington.

Gentlemen, if this unhappy concept of what appears to some to be in the public interest—as I have described it here today—were a threat to the steel industry alone, I would not have imposed upon your time and patience in this manner. But this dangerous philosophy of a profitless profit system is a grave and present menace not only to every business and industry in the land, but to the broadest possible public interest including the national security.

Unless the American people understand the true facts, and are apprised of this danger, there is little hope that they will ever be able to deal successfully with the serious inflationary problem that confronts them. I can only suggest that it is up to you—the members of the Detroit Economic Club and of similar representative organizations all over our land—and each one of you, to lay the facts before them. You have no reason or right to assume others will do the job for you.

And time is of the essence; for as the Senator from Wyoming recently said, in what I am sure was a statement of great perception (although used in a different context):

> If we destroy the free economy, we will destroy free government. That is the situation that confronts us.

And, gentlemen, it certainly is!

THE KENNEDY-IVES BILL [3]

JOHN F. KENNEDY [4]

Senator John F. Kennedy of Massachusetts gave this opening argument for Senate adoption of the Kennedy-Ives Bill, the Labor Management Reporting and Disclosure Act of 1958 (S. 3974), before the Senate on June 12, 1958.

The question of controlling labor unions was a major problem before the Eighty-fifth Congress. Senator John McClellan of Arkansas led the investigation, which began in January 1957; his committee showed that unions had abused their powers and were unable to cope with their responsibilities. A subcommittee headed by Democratic Senator Kennedy and Republican Irving Ives of New York held hearings for many months and completed its work in May 1958. The Kennedy-Ives bill provided for compulsory periodic election of union officers by democratic procedure; for full public reporting on practices involving union trusteeships; and for the barring of convicted felons from union offices.

Senator Kennedy's opening debate, interspersed with much cross-questioning, occupied most of the day. Only brief excerpts are given below. The argument was matter-of-fact, devoid of oratorical flourish; it is included in this volume as an example of the Senate solution of a problem by means of numerous amendments.

The Senate passed the bill on June 17, with 88 yeas and one negative vote. In the House the bill was voted down after limited debate. (No hearings were held, and no amendments were permitted.) Each party blamed the other for the failure. Kennedy charged that the National Association of Manufacturers had killed the bill by "misleading attacks."

After the Senate vote, Kennedy was praised not only by Democratic leader Lyndon Johnson, but also by Republican Senator Ives, who thanked Kennedy for his thoroughly bipartisan handling of the bill.

Kennedy, on this question as in other Senate debates, had a thorough knowledge of his subject. As a speaker he is relaxed, informal, candid, without a sign of a "grand manner." No orator, he even impresses his audience with seeming shyness. His style is strikingly conversational and boyishly genuine.

A strong contender for the 1960 Democratic presidential nomination, Kennedy in 1958 traveled thousands of miles in many states and delivered more than one hundred speeches, including thirty for fellow candidates. In November he was reelected with a plurality of 870,000.

[3] From text furnished by Senator John F. Kennedy. For complete text see *Congressional Record*. 104:9838-58 (daily edition). June 12, 1958.

[4] For biographical note, see Appendix.

In order that the record may be clear as we begin this debate, I would like to reply to the criticisms which have been made of the bill. Frankly, Mr. President, I fear that some who have criticized it have never taken the trouble to read it—either that or modern transatlantic communications are not up to par.

(1) It has been contended that the committee bill "would exempt from coverage more than 60 per cent of union locals." Justification for this contention is apparently based upon the claim that the cut-off of 200 members and $25,000 gross annual receipts contained in Section 101 (c) of S. 3974 constitutes "an across-the-board exemption which applies to both the reporting requirements and the regulatory provisions with respect to trusteeships and elections." This claim is completely fallacious. Section 101 (c) provides an exemption only for small unions and applies only to the reporting provisions of the bill. Even this limited exemption may be easily lifted by the Secretary if he has reason to believe that the standards of the bill are being violated. He has full investigatory authority to support his efforts, and it is expected that he would revoke any exemption where it was necessary to protect the interests of union members. It is absolutely false to say or imply that this exemption applies to reports by union officers and employers under Section 102 or 103, and it is also inaccurate to say that the regulatory provisions contained in Titles II and III with respect to trusteeships and elections are in any way affected by the exemption contained in Section 101 (c). . . .

(2) "The Western Conference of Teamsters with their Brewsters and their Becks might never be exposed to public view." Obviously this criticism is made in ignorance. The bill in Section 501 (i) (5) specifically includes "a conference, joint board, joint council . . ." in its definition of labor organizations engaged in an industry affecting commerce which are required to report under the bill. Moreover, under the Administration bill the Becks and Brewsters would not have to report conflicts of interest. Under S. 3974 a full report from union officers is required on transactions involving questionable financial dealings with employers or others which might conflict with their duties to union members.

(3) "The enforcement of the reporting requirements . . . would be almost impossible to perform inasmuch as the bill does not provide subpoena power. . ." It is true that the bill does not contain broad subpoena powers permitting the Secretary to seize records peremptorily. It does, however, contain plenary power in Sections 105 and 106 (b) and (c) to investigate, enter premises, inspect records, issue regulations, and so forth —all powers designed to more effectively enforce the statute. While I am confident that the Secretary has full powers to enforce the provisions of the bill, I would have no objection to clarifying the Secretary's powers to subpoena persons and records by an appropriate amendment to the bill.

(4) The claim has been made that the committee bill would "eliminate the requirement that unions furnish copies of their reports to the union members." This claim also is not supported by the facts. Under Section 104 (a) of the bill, the reports filed by unions would be public information. This is not the case today under the Taft-Hartley Act, even though the Senate last session passed a joint resolution authorizing the Secretary of Labor to make public the information and reports filed with him under Section 9 (f) and (g) of the Act. Under the authority the Secretary would be given by Section 104 (b) of the Committee bill, however, the Secretary could issue regulations prescribing the manner in which reports would be made available to union members. There is nothing in the bill that would compel any union member to come to Washington to obtain information contained in reports filed by his union with the Secretary. If, however, there is need to clarify this point, I would have no objection to an amendment that would require unions to furnish to each of their members the information they are required to include in their reports to the Secretary in such form and manner as the Secretary may prescribe.

(5) Criticism has implied that S. 3974 is "soft" on criminal elements which have infiltrated the labor movement. On the contrary, the bill reported by the committee would exclude the Johnny Dios and other convicted criminals from union office. It would punish with severe criminal penalties those who steal union funds. It would enable union rank and file to exercise

a secret ballot to throw crooked elements out of office, whereas the Administration bill provides no effective remedy against crooked elections. Similarly, trusteeships imposed by criminal elements to serve their own nefarious purposes could not be broken under the Administration bill. The bill before the Senate sets standards and provides machinery to eliminate improper trusteeships.

(6) Critics have alleged that the bill would destroy the present rights of union members to seek state and Federal court relief to enforce their democratic rights, continue a "no-man's land between state and Federal labor laws" and relax—and in some cases destroy—the present legal protections provided union members.

A careful reading of the bill makes clear that, except where the bill provides specifically to the contrary, union members will retain all of their present rights to seek the aid of state and Federal courts to enforce their democratic rights. The bill adds to, and does not detract from members' rights. In addition, under the bill they will have the right to invoke the aid of the Secretary of Labor and the Federal courts to relieve their locals of oppressive trusteeships maintained by national and international unions for improper or undemocratic purposes. They will also have the right and opportunity to invoke the aid of the Secretary in assuring that their constitutional officers are elected democratically by secret ballot, that members are not improperly denied the right to vote and that elections are properly conducted. . . .

(7) The complaint has been made that the committee bill "repeals the present Act's denial of access to the NLRB for failure to file financial reports." It is true that the bill does repeal Sections 9 (f) and (g) of the Taft-Hartley Act. I do not, however, regard this as a defect in the bill. On the contrary, I believe that by holding union officers and employees responsible, on pain of being subjected to criminal penalties, for the faithful discharge of their administrative duties, including honest reporting for themselves and their unions as required by the bill, and their fiduciary obligations to the members, the bill represents a distinct improvement over the Taft-Hartley Act

which penalizes the members of the union instead. Furthermore, it is a mistake to regard the procedures applicable to the selection of representatives for collective bargaining and prevention of unfair labor practices under the Taft-Hartley Act as conferring private benefits of which a union or employer can properly be deprived when they engage in certain improper conduct. These procedures have been provided to serve the public interest by enabling unions and employers to have machinery available to settle their disputes peacefully and in an orderly manner rather than by economic warfare. I do not believe that lawbreakers are induced to obey the law by placing them outside the law. On the contrary, I believe they should be made to obey the law and when they do not they should pay the penalty that the law itself provides. . . .

I regret that I have had to take the time of the Senate to correct some of the gross misstatements of fact which have been made about this bill. Not to have done so, however, would have reflected on the sincere efforts of many senators on both sides of the aisle who have worked so hard to bring before this body an effective and workable bill which will remedy the abuses disclosed by the McClellan Committee.

I could never in good conscience stand before this body and say that this is a perfect bill. In a highly complex area of legislation such as this is no bill is perfect. In an area marked as this one is by controversy and deep feeling, it is difficult indeed to report a bill with which all will agree completely. However, with the close collaboration of the ranking minority member on the subcommittee, Senator Ives, and the counsel and advice of the distinguished Senator from Arkansas, Mr. McClellan, and the diligent work of other senators on both sides of the aisle, a workable, fair, constructive and comprehensive bill which fully implements and goes beyond the legislative recommendations of the Select Committee is before the Senate. I am hopeful that it will receive the favorable consideration of this body.

FALLACIES OF LABOR CRITICISM [5]

GEORGE MEANY [6]

George Meany, president of the American Federation of Labor and Congress of Industrial Organizations, gave this special broadcast over the coast-to-coast facilities of the Columbia Broadcasting System, on October 29, 1958.

Meany's aim in this speech was to refute the major criticism hurled at labor unionism during the campaign of 1958. Especially violent were the charges and counter-charges that accompanied the voting in six states —Ohio, Kansas, Colorado, Idaho, Washington, and California—on "right-to-work" laws.

The brevity of Meany's speech gave little time for the full defense of his case. He nevertheless summarized much of his labor philosophy: (1) Labor has no desire to "take over the control of the government," a point proved by the record of labor. (2) Labor does not want to take America "down the road to socialism"; again, the record proves that American labor prefers to deal with private enterprise and that it has led the fight against communism at home and abroad. (3) Labor has supported laws to curb the power of racketeering officials. (4) Leaders of unions control no votes but their own. Unions have never officially moved into a party. Whether or not the nation-wide audience would agree with the speaker's premises and arguments, the position of labor was clearly presented, and the record was reviewed to establish his conclusions.

Meany in 1958 continued to deliver well-composed and persuasive speeches, to labor audiences and to other groups. His address in the Orange Bowl, San Bernardino, California, on April 15, was a vigorous indictment of right-to-work laws. On April 23 he addressed the Commonwealth Club of California on "American Labor in Foreign Affairs." In September he talked before the Executives' Club in Chicago, on the theme of American methods for combating the Soviet's economic challenge.

Meany's addresses are well organized, framed in the problem-solving pattern, phrased in clear and often lively language. He has many traits of the mature debater—who knows how to conciliate an audience as well as when and how to meet opposing views head on.[7]

[5] Text furnished by the American Federation of Labor and Congress of Industrial Organizations, Washington, D.C., with permission by President Meany for this reprint.

[6] For biographical note, see Appendix.

[7] For further comment on Meany as a speaker see the Cumulative **Author Index** for references to his speeches in earlier volumes.

Election time in the United States is by tradition the time for tub-thumping and breast-beating orators to point with pride and view with alarm. In accordance with that tradition all candidates for public office would have us believe that they can see nothing but sweetness and light for the nation if their party is successful and nothing but chaos, despair, misery and economic ruin if perchance the opposition party should win. Election campaigns in our country are thus characterized by extravagant statements that really insult the intelligence of the American voters.

In keeping with this rather questionable tradition we find this year's campaign following the old familiar big-lie technique with something new added.

Instead of aiming their attacks against their opponents, some politicians are trying to make labor their chief target. They are campaigning on the platform that unless they are elected, organized labor is going to take over control of the country.

The voters have been told among other things that the trade union movement has plans to socialize America as the first step toward a Communist America, that labor wants to nationalize industry in this country, that labor has plans for controlling the next Congress in order to prevent passage of legislation to curb labor racketeering and perhaps the biggest falsehood of all that the leaders of the trade union movement control the votes of the members.

This strategy of employing the high-powered lie is seldom effective in the long run, but it is always dangerous. We have learned from Hitler and Mussolini and their present counterparts in the Kremlin never to underestimate the risk of mass deception.

It is, therefore, my purpose tonight to puncture this big labor political scare balloon of 1958 with a few pointed facts.

Fact Number One can be stated simply.

Labor has no plan, nor the faintest desire, to take over control of the Government of the United States.

There is nothing in the record of the American trade union movement past or present that justifies this ridiculous contention.

No segment of American life, no group of any kind, political, economic or social is more keenly aware than is labor of the superiority of our way of life over any other form of government yet devised by the mind of man.

No group is more convinced than American labor that control of government by any special-interest group, such as organized labor, organized business, or the organized financial interests would mean an end to the American way of life.

And in my considered opinion there is no group or segment of American society which has a greater stake in the maintenance and preservation of our American system than the trade union movement.

Fact Number Two deals with another completely unfounded propaganda scare used in this campaign. For weeks the headlines have been full of charges by certain politicians that "radical labor leaders" want to take America down the road to socialism or to bring about nationalization of industry.

Labor in this country believes in free enterprise. Experience in other countries of the world shows that the worker is the real victim when free enterprise is destroyed. In my considered judgment our movement would bitterly oppose any attempt by anyone to socialize our government or to nationalize American industry.

What union leader, do you suppose, would want to trade the right to bargain freely with a private employer for the dubious privilege of going to Congress for the enactment of a law in order to raise the pay of the workers he represents?

For that matter, what union organization would be willing to surrender the right to strike against a private employer in order to deal with the government, against which a strike is out of the question?

The hidden purpose behind this cry of socialism and such phrases as leading America "down the left lane" is to plant in the minds of the American people the idea that labor is pro-Communist. This is an unforgivable and completely unjustifiable trick.

The record shows that American labor has led the fight against communism at home and abroad. Today the AFL-CIO is the nation's first line of defense against any Soviet attempt at mass subversion and infiltration here at home. President Eisenhower, himself, has publicly praised American labor for effectively checkmating Communist attempts to capture control of labor in the shops and factories of France, Italy and other free lands where, in the President's own words, "the fight was the toughest."

The fact is that the record of American labor on communism is so clear and so well known that this campaign falsehood deserves no further comment.

Now for Fact Number Three.

The charge is made, even by some in high places, that labor is going all-out politically in order to prevent passage by Congress of laws that will curb the power of a few racketeering union officials.

The record speaks most convincingly to the contrary. On its own initiative the AFL-CIO took action in accordance with its constitution to suspend and expel a number of unions found to be dominated by corrupt influences. We acted promptly and effectively on the basis of evidence brought out by the McClellan Committee after giving the accused union officials a full opportunity to refute such evidence. We acted not only against small unions but against the largest organization in the country. We did so because we firmly believe that those who betray the interests of their members, those who rob the union treasury, are the worst enemies of labor.

Incidentally what did our public officials do in the meanwhile, those armed with the power of the laws against thievery and corruption and entrusted with the duty of enforcing those laws? The record is bare of accomplishment.

And what about American business and the American bar? The McClellan Committee exposed numerous instances where businessmen were obviously corrupt in their dealings with corrupt union officials and also where lawyers who were being paid to protect the interests of the union failed to do so and actually defended and protected the interests of exploiting union officials.

Has there been any action by organized business or the American bar comparable to the action taken by organized labor? Again the record is bare.

It may be argued that present laws are inadequate to deal effectively with corruption. Again acting on its own motion, the AFL-CIO undertook to remedy such shortcomings. While we did not consider the Kennedy-Ives Bill a perfect instrument, we gave it our active support and it was passed in the Senate by an overwhelming margin. In the closing days of the last Congress, however, the bill was defeated in the House of Representatives.

Now we find some brazen campaign orators daring to claim that passage of the bill in the House was blocked by "radical labor bosses."

These hypocritical politicians must be relying on the proverbial short memory of the public. Is it possible they have forgotten in a few short weeks that it was actually the National Association of Manufacturers, the Chamber of Commerce and other big business interests who helped to kill the measure and boasted about it afterward? And why? Simply because the bill contained restrictions against corrupt activities by corporation officials as well as union officials.

I do not believe in calling the kettle black. I will never defend union racketeering. But it should be pointed out that every time a union officer goes bad, you are apt to find one or more employers who gave him bribes because they considered it more expedient to deal with a union representative they had bought and paid for rather than with an honest union leader.

Let me emphasize that labor will support legislation to curb malpractices by union and corporation officials in the next Congress, just as we did in the last Congress.

Now for Fact Number Four.

The leaders of American unions insofar as I can judge from many years of experience do not control any vote but their own.

Speaking for myself I can assure you that I control only my own vote. I would strongly resent any one trying to control or dictate to me as to how I should vote and I know the American worker too well to believe for one minute that he would allow his precious right to vote to be compromised or controlled by any one.

Bear in mind that the membership of the AFL-CIO is made up of Americans. Just look around you, see for yourself who are the members of our unions. The postman who delivers your mail; the clerk who checks you out at the supermarket; the thousands who crowd the roads of our nation each morning on their way to work in our giant industrial enterprises; the building trade worker who builds your homes; the railroad worker who serves you on a cross-country trip or who brings you into town from the suburbs; the airline pilots and crews who criss-cross America with thousands of flights every day; the men and women who wait upon you in our hotels and restaurants; the teachers who teach your children; the tens of thousands of workers who produce your radios, TV's, tires, as well as the vital weapons for our nation's defense; the actors you see on stage or on the motion picture screen; the man who sits next to you in church or at the PTA meeting; your neighbor across the street, these are the members of America's unions—Americans all, every last one of them. Look them over, talk to them, judge for yourself. Is any union leader or anyone else going to control their vote?

The thought may well occur to some that because I state labor is not trying to run the country or to socialize or nationalize industry or control Congress that I am trying to convey the impression that labor is not active politically. Let me assure you that I have no such intention.

Labor is active politically, has been for many years and is today more active in this field than ever before.

Why? For two major reasons.

First, in self-defense. Under the Taft-Hartley Act, adopted by Congress in 1947, states were given the right to prohibit any form of union security in labor-management contracts. By means of an intensive propaganda campaign, the voters of eighteen states have since been prevailed upon to enact such prohibitions, masquerading under the name of "right-to-work laws." The same misleading proposition is on the ballot in six more states this year.

These so-called right-to-work laws grant no one an actual right to work. They create not a single new job. A worker receives merely the "right not to join a union" in a plant where the majority of the workers want a union. This has all the attraction and value of the "right not to eat" and the "right not to get a living wage."

The real aim and effect of the right-to-work laws is to weaken and destroy the bargaining powers of workers. As individuals, workers are helpless against the concentrated economic power of big corporations. They can find protection and security only through strong and secure trade unions which are outlawed by right-to-work laws.

Labor has been forced, therefore, to become more active in politics in order to expose the sham of the misnamed right-to-work laws and to elect candidates who oppose such harmful legislation.

The second reason for labor's increased political activity is broader and more fundamental. It goes back to the early days of the trade union movement when Samuel Gompers and his colleagues fought for and won universal free education for the nation's children . . . the eight-hour-day law and workmen's compensation.

They realized even back in the 1890's that human progress is not limited to economic advances won through collective bargaining, important as they are—that vital social objectives can be achieved in a free nation like ours only through legislative action by the elected representatives of the people.

Following that philosophy, the labor movement helped to win enactment of social security, unemployment insurance, slum clearance, bank deposit insurance and many other reforms, all of which were denounced years ago as socialistic. Would anyone seriously consider abandoning these safeguards today? Have they injured, or have they reinforced, our free way of life?

This year we are working hard again to elect liberal and progressive candidates from both parties to the next Congress. Why? Because we expect them to take orders from us? Ridiculous! We would not have any respect for that type of public official. Candidates gain our support only when they themselves consistently support progressive legislation, regardless of pressure from party leaders or *any other source.*

What do we mean by progressive legislation?

We mean construction of thousands of new schools to wipe out our national educational deficit. Isn't that something all the American people want?

We mean action to restore industrial prosperity, to end mass unemployment, create millions of new jobs each year for our young people as they graduate from school. Action like home building, road building as well as school building. Can anyone deny our country needs such action?

We mean modernization of social security and unemployment insurance to prevent needless human suffering—broadening of minimum wage coverage so that millions of the lowest paid workers can rise above starvation standards. Is that too ambitious a goal in a nation as wealthy as ours?

We want the government to fill the gaping holes in our national defense structure. Can we afford to run a poor second to Soviet Russia in missiles and rockets through a suicidal policy of false economy?

We want courageous action, once and for all, to accord equal civil rights to all citizens, regardless of race, color or religion. How else can we maintain effective leadership in the world struggle for the survival of freedom and human justice?

These are programs that will benefit not only union members, but all Americans. We are proud to work for them and to give our support to candidates who are willing to vote for them. We rest our case with the American people with full confidence in the verdict they will render on November 4.

LABOR'S RESPONSIBILITY FOR HUMAN RIGHTS [8]

DAVID J. MCDONALD [9]

David J. McDonald, president of the United Steelworkers of America, gave this address on February 3, 1958, at the National Conference for Human Rights, at the Bellevue-Stratford Hotel, Philadelphia. The conference was co-sponsored by McDonald and George M. Leader, Governor of Pennsylvania. Speakers preceding McDonald were Governor Leader and Joseph J. Morrow, personnel director of Pitney-Bowes, Inc.

President of the Steelworkers since 1953, when he succeeded the late Philip Murray, McDonald was often categorized as a "labor conservative" with chief concern for the economic issues of unionism. In his inaugural address he asserted that "democratic capitalism, combined with industrial democracy, is unquestionably the best way of life for mankind."

McDonald's record in national and international labor affairs has been impressive. He served on the Commission on Foreign Economic Policy (1953); was active in the National Recovery Administration with Murray; led in the organization of American and Canadian steelworkers; was a delegate to study labor problems in Latin America under the sponsorship of the Office of Inter-American Affairs (1943); served in many government agencies during World War II; helped form the International Confederation of Trade Unions; and served as special assistant to Eric Johnston, director of the Economic Stabilization Administration.

As a speaker McDonald is fluent, ready, dynamic. At Holy Cross High School, at Duquesne University in Pittsburgh, and at the Drama School of the Carnegie Institute of Technology, he developed much oral skill. In his thirty years with Murray, McDonald steadily improved in his ability in informal discussion as well as in platform leadership.

McDonald opened the ninth biennial constitutional convention of the Unted Steelworkers, at Atlantic City, in September 1958. The occasion was a fiery one that challenged his leadership. Calling for united resistance to an opposing faction led by Donald Rarick, McDonald in the give-and-take debate crushed his opponents. Demanding substantial improvements in wages, hours, and fringe benefits for the new contract, he said, "You cannot be weak and divided if you want to enjoy fewer hours of work per day and per week."

[8] Text from *Proceedings of a National Conference for Human Rights,* Philadelphia, February 1958. Reprinted here by permission of David J. McDonald. Text, with slight variations, also reprinted in *Congressional Record.* 104:A1881-2 (daily edition). February 28, 1958.

[9] For biographical note, see Appendix.

I want to express my appreciation to everybody who has come here today to join with Governor Leader and me and my colleagues in this National Conference for Human Rights.

It is indeed rewarding to know that so many prominent leaders of our national community, representing almost every facet of American life, have been willing to take this time from their very busy lives to help make this Conference a historic occasion, a historic step to what I believe is America's progressive effort to solve the problems of human relations.

I think you all will agree this is a novel experiment, perhaps the first of its kind to be conducted under the auspices of the government of a great industrial state and the leadership of a large labor union.

The problems for which we seek solutions affect the lives of every citizen in our country and are in some way related to the things that affect the people who live in all other countries of the world.

Governor Leader and Mr. Morrow have spoken on the responsibilities of government and industry in the business of protecting human rights. I am going to try to outline what I believe to be labor's role in this particular field.

The whole broad subject of human relations and the protection of human rights is one that labor must of necessity give attention to every day. It is broad in the sense that we are obligated to negotiate contracts with employers which incorporate within their framework certain provisions which govern wages, hours and conditions of employment. In essence, these contracts provide equality of treatment for all employees regardless of race, creed, color or national origin.

And within this framework we have made real progress, particularly during the last twenty years. During this period the American trade union movement has grown from 3.5 million to over 17 million members. It is obvious that these workers are now in a position to include provisions in their agreements which will guarantee equality of treatment for all people under the contract.

And, of course, it is significant to note that in our own union, the United Steelworkers of America, racial and intergroup relations have continued to improve from year to year as the workers' economic status has improved.

It is also significant that there have never been any outbreaks due to racial conflict in any of the plants where we have labor contracts. And this, in spite of the fact that serious breakdowns in race relations have occurred in the very communities where the plants are located.

I am justly proud of what we have done to date to free the steelworker from the economic and social restrictions which combine to prevent the full enjoyment of a happy life.

I would like to enumerate some of these accomplishments.

(1) We have established equal pay for equal work in the steel industry, regardless of race, creed, color or national origin.

(2) The North-South wage differential which existed for so many years has been eliminated.

(3) We have negotiated pension and insurance plans which permit steelworkers to retire under conditions providing substantial financial security, regardless of race, creed, color or national origin.

(4) We have developed educational facilities for training our members to assume the responsibilities of holding local union offices and for participating in community service work.

(5) Our Committee on Civil Rights, which was created in 1948, has played an important role in carrying the union's policy and program against discrimination into the local, state and national community. It has promoted a program within the union to prepare our members for dealing with the multitude of human relations problems which are a part of everyday union life. We have no segregated locals and many Negroes hold local union office. They are holding positions of great importance in our organization not because of the fact that they are Negroes, but because of the fact that they have demonstrated their ability to hold these offices.

(6) Enforcement of the union's basic policy of equal rights and representation has opened up many categories of employment heretofore closed to members of minority groups. Moreover, regional progress is now being made to establish on-the-job

apprentice training programs in the crafts (which Mr. Morrow has made reference to) giving people an opportunity to rise up through these apprentice training programs.

(7) Union support and guidance has played an important part in the enactment of fair employment practices legislation in fifteen states and forty cities, the majority of which are located in heavily industrialized areas.

(8) We have participated in almost one hundred district and national conferences on matters of human relations since 1954. We are affiliated with twenty-five state and national committees and organizations whose programs on human rights, civil rights and civil liberties conform to the policy of the United Steelworkers of America.

(9) Our nationally televised monthly union meetings have served to direct public attention to many of the things we are here to discuss today.

You now have some idea of what we have been doing in the field of human rights and civil liberties. But we do not propose to stand on our record. Up to now we have attacked only the fringes of the problem as it affects the average citizen.

It is largely true that segregation ends when men and women enter the mill or the factory for there is literally no segregation in a mill or a factory. And for that we feel that the energies that we have expended have not been in vain.

But the other sixteen hours of a man's day are also important. Constitutionally and psychologically can a man be expected to work equally if he is not permitted to eat equally, reside equally, relax equally, improve his knowledge equally, play equally, travel equally—in short, if he is not permitted to live equally?

This is where we are falling short in America. This is the chink in our armor. Compassionate people everywhere feel the pull of this tainted weight. But the need for action has not manifested itself in those who are right-thinking and compassionate. And unless it does, we will not carry out our purpose.

Unions have their frailties—and that includes the United Steelworkers—because they are human in nature and in character. Just as human as the leaders in the business world, and in religion, and education, and other walks of life.

There is still too much idle talk about what kind of a country we should have and the way society should be organized, and too little done in the practical application of the things which make freedom and justice meaningful.

I do not mean to infer that any one segment of our society is solely responsible for our failure to measure up to our role as leader among the democratic nations of the world.

For while I am the nominal head of a strong trade union numbering about a million and a quarter men and women, I would be guilty of misrepresentation if I said there was complete unanimity of opinion among all our members on the subject of human rights. Unfortunately, we still have in our union those who get quite worked up about equality of opportunity, and they get quite vocal about this subject, but they never practice it themselves.

We haven't been able to break down completely employment practices and community patterns which still deny minority members of our union the opportunity to work and live as full-fledged, law-abiding citizens. But we are trying.

Let me say with emphasis that the United Steelworkers of America and other great unions have dedicated themselves to the orderly attainment of equality of opportunity for all Americans. We are pledged to work for the elimination of discrimination in all its ugly manifestations and the prejudices upon which it feeds. We are going to attain this goal if it is humanly possible to do so. And to this we dedicate ourselves.

But while the responsibility of the forces of labor in America looms large in this enterprise, ours is not the sole responsibility. We have done what we have done because we believe in the Fatherhood of God, the Brotherhood of Man, the tenets of the constitutions of our union and of the United States.

I have said this before, and I say it again today, that the National Association of Manufacturers and the National Chamber of Commerce, together with the local bodies of these associations, must speak out firmly and give their support for compliance with the Supreme Court's ban on segregation, for fair practices in employment and in housing, and in support of legislation which will guarantee all Americans equal protection under the law.

And I would like to call upon those who formulate the policies of the great industries of America to use their wide influence to help set the pattern in which these things can be realized. I think the leaders of American industry can do this far better even than the leaders of labor.

The policy and administrative procedures under which industry operates are largely made in the North. It is the obligation of those who formulate and enforce these policies to institute an educational program for management personnel so that they can join with us in helping to establish real American democracy in the North as well as in the South.

We have already shown that all categories of men work well together if given a chance. With the help of industry, we can make the mills and factories of this country the real classrooms of democracy.

If we are losing our prestige and our position of leadership among the countries of the world, we can attribute it in part to the fact that we have failed to avail ourselves of the tremendous human resources we have at our disposal.

In the light of our failure to practice what we preach, people in other countries tend to forget the things that are truly America. They forget the magnificent contributions of individual initiative and cooperative enterprise. They forget the engineering and scientific skills that have made our way of life the goal of all men. They forget the enormous economic assistance we have poured into their countries. And they forget that this nation, twice in the past half century, has risen up as one to help defeat potential world dictatorship. They prefer to look at our weaknesses.

Our treatment of minorities is one of the chief obstacles we face in our efforts to achieve world peace. World peace is a moral ideal and our highest political ambition. It can be established only on the basis of high moral principle.

A nation's morals is not conjured up in legislative halls and judicial chambers. Morals is a substantive thing, rooted deep in the lives and homes of every citizen. On a moral issue, in world council, our diplomats can be only as effective as the moral standards of the people they represent. Consequently, our elected and appointed government officials in their efforts toward world peace are being hamstrung by our national attitude toward minorities.

If we are losing the battle in the court of world opinion on this point, what is the effect upon ourselves here at home?

I believe that race and religious prejudices are a cancer on our social, economic and political fortunes. The problem of the Negro is especially acute. Negroes unwanted in the South are moving to the North where they are equally unwanted. School districts in many parts of the country are being gerrymandered to assure the separation of whites and nonwhites. Newly-built suburban developments are restrictively white. Older urban sections are filled to overflowing with nonwhite and foreign-born—through their sheer inability to go elsewhere.

No Negro in America has full social, economic and political freedom. He may acquire one, or even two, of these freedoms but never all three. The Civil War made his political freedom attainable. FEPC laws make a stab at economic freedom. One doubts that social freedom can ever be legislated.

The northerner takes a smug attitude as he ponders the Negro situation in the South. But he has nothing to be smug about. To all intents and purposes, there is as much segregation in the North as there is in the South. In general, the northerner accepts the Negro as a race but not as an individual. In the South the Negro is accepted as an individual, but not as a race. From a Negro's point of view he is as bad off in one section as another.

In spite of all the serious questions that demand our attention today, the problem of racial minorities is still our number one problem, as it was ninety-five years ago when the Emancipation Proclamation was signed.

We have failed to meet the challenge of building good human relations and establishing strong moral values, in keeping with our unprecedented material and technological progress.

In failing to provide equality of opportunity and equal protection under the law for all Americans, we have contributed to a tragic waste of manpower, talent, intellectual and moral energy, all of which are so necessary if our nation is to continue to progress and to remain strong.

Our crying need today is for strong, courageous, intelligent leadership which realizes that we face the most weighty problem of the century, a problem so complex that it can only be dealt with by men and women who are dedicated to the principles of justice and freedom.

As the leaders of American culture, religion, education, industry, labor and affairs of state, we have willingly or unwillingly inherited this responsibility. It is ours. The problem is here, now, and it is alive, and it needs immediate attention.

We in labor accept our responsibility. Some measures we can take alone, and we will take them. In others, we will need the help of everyone gathered here today and all of your constituencies.

In brief, let me review our union's program:

(1) We propose to set up a million-dollar-a-year scholarship reservoir. These scholarships will not be restricted to science and engineering, but will embrace a wide range of educational opportunity. Students will be selected from every walk of life without regard to race, color, religion or national origin.

(2) We propose to select representatives from our membership to visit NATO nations as ambassadors of good will.

(3) We propose to work out a program with industry which will insure upgrading the qualified employees without respect to their creed, color or national origin. We propose to broaden the in-plant training programs for apprentices to qualify members of minority groups to work in presently restricted categories.

(4) We shall expand opportunities in the union for minorities, making more positions of leadership available.

(5) We shall support demands for Federal aid and finance for additional aid to education and equal educational opportunities.

(6) We propose to work more closely with community leaders in broadening the influence of minority groups.

(7) We shall support a program to abolish slums and provide badly needed low-cost and middle-income homes.

(8) We propose to see to it that all citizens are accorded equal protection and justice under the law.

Because we believe these eight points are sound, reasonable, honest and worthy of attainment, we pledge ourselves to their fulfillment.

Never before have so many influential leaders met to deal with this grave and urgent problem. Is it too much to hope that we will do more toward solving the problem than at any other event in our history?

The spelling out of precepts and a heightened understanding of human relations by leaders are only the preliminary step toward achieving the objectives we discuss today. But we all have a solemn obligation to convert sound precept into effective practice among those we represent.

The opportunity is ours.

In the words of my good friend, Dr. Howard McClusky, at our first human relations seminar at Penn State University in 1951:

> No one knows how much time we have, but it can't be long. It would be fatal to assume that somehow we will muddle through our inhumanities into some form of ultimate accommodation. Fate will not be so kind. On the contrary, it must be the responsibility of free men of good will to work increasingly for satisfying relations among people everywhere
>
> It would not be extravagant to hope that the experience and example of our meeting here today will contribute materially to that goal.

Please God, let it be so.

NATIONAL POLITICS

VOTE REPUBLICAN [1]

RICHARD M. NIXON [2]

Vice President Richard M. Nixon gave this political campaign address at Indianapolis, Indiana, on September 29, 1958. The occasion was a one-hundred-dollar-a-plate dinner to raise money for the Republican campaign and to support Governor Harold V. Handley, candidate for the seat in the United States Senate vacated by Republican Senator W. E. Jenner.

The speech was in Nixon's campaign manner of the 1952, 1954, and 1956 campaigns. In his speaking in 1958, he had a more decisive "in-fighting" method than in the 1956 campaign. Nixon met head on the Democratic attacks on the Eisenhower policies and made the November election a choice between a vote of confidence in the Eisenhower Administration and surrender to the wild-spending radical branch of the Democrats (the ADA wing). This argument, typically political, minimized Democratic support in the enactment of the President's most cherished programs of foreign aid and trade and national defense.

An indefatigable campaigner in October 1958, Nixon covered eastern and central states and especially California and the Far West. Everywhere he attacked the Truman Administration as having done nothing to stop inflation. As always his delivery and platform aggressiveness were impressive. His numerous platform radio and television appearances since 1956 had given him more maturity and ease before audiences. Without question he was the leading Republican stump speaker during the 1958 political battle.

In 1959 Vice President Nixon, partly as a result of his most vigorous campaigning, continued to have the strong backing of organization Republicans as a presidential nominee. But the 1958 Democratic landslide in California and Nelson A. Rockefeller's New York gubernatorial plurality of some 560,000 over Democratic Averell Harriman inevitably affected Nixon's standing in the race for the Republican nomination in 1960.[3]

I am delighted that again as in 1956 I am making my first speech of this campaign in my mother's home state of Indiana. It would be natural for me to say this in view of the fact that

[1] Text supplied by Vice President Richard M. Nixon, with permission for this reprint.

[2] For biographical note, see Appendix.

[3] For further comment on Nixon as a speaker see the Cumulative Author Index for references to his speeches in earlier volumes.

1956 proved to be a winning campaign. But this year in particular I am glad to be with you because if there is one thing you can be sure of it is that Indiana's Republicans are full of fight.

As a matter of fact, you like to fight so much that you have a few good fights among yourselves. But you can always be counted upon to get together against your Democratic opponents in a final campaign. And one thing is certain—you don't put your tail between your legs and run because things look bad. . . .

By whatever tests—peace, prosperity, honesty—this Administration has done a better job than its predecessor, and it deserves the support of the American people.

With this kind of a record, why is it then that the Republican party seems to be in trouble in this election? Some put the blame on the fact that Republicans are divided. It is said that some want to cut the budget and some add to it. Some favor foreign aid—some are against it. Some Republicans are modern and some are old-fashioned.

Let us recognize that there are differences among Republicans just as there should and will be in any party which is one of a two-party system. But when you consider our differences, remember that they are small compared to the differences which divide the Democrats. And also, and far more important, our differences are infinitesimal when you consider the gulf between the principles in which most Republicans believe and those held by the radical ADA wing which dominates the Democratic National Committee today.

Here we come to the key issues of this campaign. We say elect more Republicans and assure continuation of the policies of our Republican President and his Administration. They say elect more Democrats so that those policies can be changed.

What changes will they make? To answer this question we must find the answer to another one. If more Democrats are elected, what kind of Democrats will they be? To which Democratic party will they belong?

They will not come from the conservative southern wing of the party. Newly-elected Democrats will come from the radical ADA wing which controls the party in the northern and western states. Because these are the states in which the key contests for control of the House and the Senate are being fought out.

What will electing more Democrats of the ADA radical type mean? Let me answer that question by asking what you want from government. Do you want to cut government spending?

Here is what you would get if more Democrats are elected this year. The budget for this year is $5 billion larger than it would have been because of bills voted by the Democratic-controlled Congress over the amounts requested by the President. In addition, the President vetoed bills which would have added another $1.5 billion to our deficit.

And Democrats in the last Congress introduced bills which would cost $206.5 billion over the next five years in addition to the amounts planned by the Administration. One senator alone, Proxmire of Wisconsin, introduced five bills in the last Congress which would cost by his own estimate $35 billion over a five-year period.

You can see what you would get if more senators of that philosophy are elected this November. You will be in for a wild spending binge by radical Democrats, drunk with visions of votes and not pink but dead elephants.

What would this mean? This means that when you vote for more Democrats in the House and Senate you are voting to raise your taxes, cheapen your money, and to stifle the new investment and enterprise which means more jobs and more progress for the American people.

Do you want to control labor racketeering? You can kiss goodby any chance for effective labor legislation if you increase the number of those Democratic congressmen and senators who will owe their election to contributions and support of the very labor politicians they are supposed to control. Because remember, labor politicians don't give support unless they get 100 per cent domination of the man they help to elect.

Do you want to resist the trend to big government? By electing more of the radical ADA type of Democrats to the House and Senate, you can be sure that a flood of bills will be introduced with the object of moving toward the nationalization of health, housing, power, farming and other American institutions. Because these radical ADA-type Democrats honestly and sincerely believe that government enterprise is superior to private enterprise in providing for the needs of the people.

What does all this add up to? America has had its greatest progress in history in the last six years because we have had an Administration in Washington that has recognized that there is only one sure way to progress, one sure way to get the schools, the highways, the hospitals, the security that we all want. That way is through government policy which encourages and unleashes the creative energies of 170 million individual Americans and which further recognizes that government action in any area is justified only when individuals will not or cannot do what needs to be done for themselves.

Our progress can continue if we continue that policy. But if we go back to the bankrupt ideas of the New and Fair Deals which failed to produce prosperity and peace in twenty years, you will stop America's progress in its tracks.

The issue, very simply stated, is this—guarantee progress for America by electing more Republicans. Stop progress by electing more Democrats. This issue is bigger than any division in the Republican party. It is bigger than any differences between Republicans and Democrats. It is as big as America itself.

I have traveled to fifty-five countries in the last six years as a representative of the President and of the American people. I have seen many kinds of government policies in operation in that period. And every time I return to the United States I realize how fortunate we are to live in this country. We can lose what we have if we don't fight for it—work for it and vote for it.

That is why I ask you to join me tonight and to go forth and tell this story so that we can win a victory not just for the Republican party but for America.

PRINCIPLES OF THE DEMOCRATIC PARTY[4]

HARRY S. TRUMAN[5]

Former President Harry S. Truman gave this political address before three thousand Democratic diners in Washington, D.C., on February 22, 1958. The occasion, a one-hundred-dollar-a-plate fund-raising dinner at the Sheraton Park Hotel, was the climax of two days of party business that aimed at the continued control of Congress in the 1958 elections and victory in 1960. Adlai Stevenson and prominent Democratic congressional leaders also addressed the audience.

The seventy-three-year-old main speaker dominated the overflowing audience with his old-time speaking liveliness and political aggressiveness. His ideas and language were reminiscent of his political stump speaking during his heyday ten years earlier. He accused the Administration of five years of "economic misrule" and asserted that the American people were "tired of being bamboozled," were "fed up with Republican hucksters and their campaign oratory," and with their "liberal pep-talks and reactionary policies." He gave a graphic catalogue of Republican shortcomings, and developed five principles that his "party of the people" is to follow. With loyalty to such principles, political victory would be assured and the Republic would "regain the confidence of the world."[6]

The most terrifying result of this five-year period of Republican complacency . . . is that the Soviet Union has been determinedly driving ahead with all the fierce energy that a dictatorship can command, while we have slipped backward in relative strength.

We have been slashing our conventional armed forces year by year. We have failed to bring our weapons up to date, and we have failed to go full speed ahead in the development of new weapons and missiles. . . .

Democrats have been pointing out this dangerous lag ever since 1953, when one of the new Administration's first acts was to chop $5 billion off the expansion of the Air Force. But these

[4] Excerpt from text printed in the New York *Times,* February 23, 1958, p46. A copy was also furnished by former President Truman.

[5] For biographical note, see Appendix.

[6] For further comment on Truman as a speaker, see the Cumulative Author Index for references to his speeches in earlier volumes.

Democratic protests were voiced in vain until the two Russian satellites went into orbit around the globe.

Up to that point, the answer to any criticism of our military policy had always been that we have a general in the White House, and when it comes to national defense, a general must be right. Well, the Sputniks woke the people up.

Now, what should the Democratic party do in this present state of affairs?

These are the principles that should guide us:

First, the Democratic party is, and must remain, the party of the people. Our primary concern is with the vast majority who make the backbone of the nation—the working men and women, farmers, people on salary, and people of moderate incomes. We are, of course, also concerned with the welfare of the well-to-do; and I have noticed that in the long run they, too, seem to fare better under the Democrats than under the Republicans. But we should always make sure it can be said of us, "The Democratic party is better for the little fellow."

The second Democratic principle is that the Democratic party must stand firmly and forthrightly for the full enjoyment and protection of the civil rights and liberties of every citizen in the land regardless of race, creed, or national origin. I think that firm and foresighted leadership might accomplish this without calling on the Army for help.

Indeed, I know that patient and persistent action, coupled with firmness, can work wonders in the field of civil rights. But unless a President works at it, day and night, and shows the people where he stands, you can expect the demagogues to move in and make trouble. Be that as it may, for the Democratic party there can be no compromise which will deny to any of our people the enjoyment of their basic rights of citizenship.

Democratic principle Number Three: The Democratic party must believe in, and work for, a constant economic growth and a rising standard of living. Progress is an article of faith with us. We believe that our economy can continue to grow steadily year after year, producing more and more goods and services for more and more people—and that there is no inevitable law of nature that requires periodic downturns where everyone is "put through the wringer."

Moreover, we believe the government has a considerable measure of responsibility for creating conditions in which steady economic growth will take place. The Democratic party must be prepared to fulfill that responsibility completely and should constantly develop plans and programs to that end.

Democratic principle Number Four: In foreign policy, the Democratic party must stand firmly for cooperation and concerted action with other free nations. The business of working with allies from many lands, allies who have varied interests and diverse points of view, is always difficult and complex—and is frequently exasperating. But in the world of today there is no acceptable alternative.

The contest between our free way of life and the totalitarian system of the Communist bloc is a grave challenge to the continued existence of the United States as a sovereign nation and to our continued existence as free men. This is a contest we cannot afford to lose. And in the long run, it is likely to be determined by the economic strength and industrial power of the contending forces arrayed on either side.

Today, the free nations together have a preponderance of economic strength, but the United States cannot go it alone. It requires the cooperation of the whole free world to maintain our economic and military superiority. Russia and her satellites are gaining rapidly in strength. The free nations have an extremely tough struggle even if we stick together. If we fall apart, we can only expect the worst.

International cooperation must be not only the watchword of our foreign policy, it must also be the central theme of our whole national life—shaping our course in everything we do, domestic as well as foreign.

Democratic principle Number Five: The Democratic party must support an adequate national defense, whatever the cost. There are some basic facts everyone ought to understand in order to see this problem in the proper perspective. For one thing, there is the fact that our struggle with communism is a life-and-death struggle. We hope and pray that this struggle can be settled by peaceful means, but we know the Russians will settle it by conquest—if they can.

We are dealing here with the question of our survival. Modern weapons are so terrible we cannot assure our survival with certainty no matter what we do. But the best chance of survival is the maintenance, with our allies, of the strongest possible defense system. This is very, very expensive in terms of money. When we come to decide whether or not we are willing to pay the price, the question is not, "What is it convenient for us to pay?" Rather, the question is, "What is it worth to survive?"

The answer of the Democratic party must be clear and unequivocal: We are prepared to devote to our survival all our wealth and resources that are needed and can be effectively used for that purpose.

Remember the last sentence in the Declaration of Independence:

> And for the support of this declaration, with a firm reliance on Divine Providence, we mutually pledge to each other our lives, our fortunes and our sacred honor.

Remember this too, my friends—mere survival is not our only concern. How we survive is far more important—whether we survive as free men and a nation unafraid—or as a cowering, frightened people in retreat. We must do what is necessary to survive as a free people, no matter what the cost.

Indeed, I do not see how any man, whatever his politics, who has the courage to face the facts, and the sense to understand them, could arrive at any other answer. But apparently some people—people in high places—have arrived at a different answer and are now basing our national policy upon it. Or perhaps it would be more accurate to say that they really have not arrived at any answer and that we have no national policy on this vital question—except to follow the line of least resistance. Again, it may be that they have not arrived at the right answer because they have not even asked themselves the right question.

I hope, my friends, that as we get on about our business of winning the elections in 1958 and then the presidential election in 1960, we will hold fast to these fundamental principles. Some of the principles may seem popular; some may not. But because they are right, we must stick to them, remembering that, in the long run, good government is good politics, and the best government is the best politics. If we don't do what we know is right, we don't deserve to win. Let's go ahead on that basis, and we will come out all right.

These principles will dispel the fears of the American people and justify the hopes they have placed in us. With these principles, we can win resounding majorities in Congress in 1958 and the presidency in 1960. With these principles, this great Republic will regain the confidence of the world in our ability to lead the way to peace, freedom and security.

INAUGURAL ADDRESS[7]

NELSON A. ROCKEFELLER[8]

On January 1, 1959, Nelson A. Rockefeller gave this inaugural address as forty-ninth governor of New York. It was a fourteen-minute speech in the crowded Assembly chamber. The occasion was less demonstrative than that of four years before at the inauguration of Governor Averell Harriman.

The new Governor emphasized the close relation between New York's problems and those of the nation and the world. He dedicated himself to enlarging man's opportunities everywhere in a world of peace. He touched significantly on such problems as the South's resistance to school integration; the civil rights issue; and the need for economic progress and expansion. He decried the tendency to label men politically and said that he was "liberal, conservative, and progressive." Once only, when he referred to "free men everywhere," was he interrupted by applause.

The address reflected principles and attitudes that no doubt evoked warm response from the rank and file of American citizens. The New York *Times* editorially pronounced the speech as "a state paper touched with eloquence, perhaps with greatness."

Rockefeller's spectacular campaign and election in 1958 aroused immediate speculation that he might be a Republican presidential contender in 1960. His personality, enthusiasm, youthful vigor (his age was fifty), sense of humor, organizational ability, social outlook were qualities noted. It was observed too that his was a Bible-reading family; that he had attended the progressive Lincoln School of Columbia University; that he was graduated from Dartmouth College, with a Phi Beta Kappa award; that he had helped to promote the rental of Rockefeller buildings; that he had served as coordinator of Latin American affairs in the Department of State; that he had helped frame President Truman's Point Four Program; and that he had worked within and without the government on international economic aid programs. Rockefeller's Albany address was an effective climax to this record in business, international service, and politics.

As this sixth decade of our twentieth century nears its end, we are nearing, too, what could be the fatal testing time for free men—and freedom itself—everywhere.

[7] Text supplied by Richard Amper, press secretary to Governor Nelson Rockefeller, with the Governor's permission for this reprint.

[8] **For biographical note, see Appendix.**

Over the span of many a century, many a generation thinks its own age is a moment of historic decision. We know it.

We know it because we have witnessed—for more than twenty-five years now—the tragic ordeal of freedom. We have seen the tyrant—first Fascist, then Communist—strike down free nations, shackle free peoples, and dare free men everywhere to prove they can survive.

We know this to be such a time of historic decision, because we see the world divided, the weapons of war perfected to deadly extremes, and humanity seeming, at times, about to turn and prey upon itself.

And we know something else: we know how and why this world is divided and imperiled.

It is divided, essentially, between those who believe in the brotherhood of men under the fatherhood of God—and those who scorn this as a pious myth.

It is divided between those who believe in the dignity of free men—and those who believe in the monstrous supremacy of the totalitarian state.

It is divided between those whose most potent force is their faith in individual freedom—and those whose faith is force itself.

It is divided between those who believe in the essential equality of peoples of all nations and races and creeds—and those whose only creed is their own ruthless race for power.

This division of the world—and this time of decision—leave no corner of the earth, no fraction of humanity, untouched. From this basic struggle, there can be no refuge, nor escape.

Our neighborhood is the world. History and technology, the hope of free man everywhere and the menace to freedom everywhere: all things have conspired to make this so. The speed of the rocket and the force of an atom bomb, the strength of America and the strength of her enemies: such things mean that every state in our union, every community in our state, every citizen in each community—all face a common challenge and share a common cause.

The graveness of the challenge is matched by the greatness of our opportunity to serve this common cause.

Knowing this, we have no reason to fear—but every reason to strive.

For the spiritual resources of free men are unique, and the strength of free men is unsurpassed—if united in common purpose. Our history itself, as a people, is living and lasting testimony to this. As a nation, we were born of a free association of individuals—a concord of states—joining with one another in the modern world's most astonishing story of national adventure and creation: the stirring story of America. In the same spirit and on a wider horizon, the twenty-one American republics of this Western Hemisphere, freely joined in common purpose and in friendship, have given practical demonstration of their dedication to peace and human dignity. Today throughout the world such free associations of free peoples, working together in their mutual interests, can achieve the universal aspiration of man for individual opportunity.

From the individual's faith in his own worth, to his voluntary role in his own free community, to his own community's service to his nation, and to his nation's dedication to the common cause of all free men—thus is the force of the faith of freedom steadily raised to a higher power.

And as we know the strength of this faith, we know, too, there is still further reason for confidence and courage in the material means and devices we can employ to serve this faith. For the first time in history, the revolution of science and industry makes possible the realization of man's ageless dream of individual opportunity and well-being. The commonwealth of humanity at large can be served now as never before in the story of man. Disease can be conquered. The hungry can be fed. The homeless can find shelter. Such things can come to pass in a measure no earlier generation of man has dared imagine.

Through these means can we serve, as no other age has served, the true end of freedom: not merely checking menace and peril to free peoples—but assuring to free men of all nations the chance to nourish their spirit, enrich their mind, each to live a life of promise true to his chosen destiny.

I speak to you today—obviously—as citizens of America and of the free world.

We can serve—and save—freedom elsewhere only as we practice it in our own lives.

We cannot speak of the equality of men and nations unless we hold high the banner of social equality in our own communities.

We cannot speak of a rule of law among nations of the world unless our own laws faithfully serve the needs, and guard the rights, of our own citizens.

We cannot be impressively concerned with the needs of impoverished peoples in distant lands, if our own citizens are left in want.

We cannot hope to spur economic progress and prosperity in the world unless such a state as New York can itself help to lead America herself toward new horizons of well-being and equal opportunity for all our citizens.

We cannot pretend to help inspire new young nations in the ways of freedom and its institutions—if our schools do not enable our own youth to be enlightened citizens.

We cannot hope to serve the cause of peace among nations—if classes or factions in our own society war among themselves.

Thus does our role in the world—and our duty to ourselves—coincide as if they were one. We are called upon to conduct ourselves like free men—with the will and the wisdom to make freedom work.

We do this not with rhetoric—but with action. We do this not simply by what we say—but by how we live.

We must speed our economic growth—for upon the vitality of our economy depend jobs and incomes for all. We must help industry prosper and expand. We must face realistically our transportation problems. We must wisely develop our natural resources. For only in all such ways can we guard our truly priceless resources: our citizens and their well-being.

We must make more orderly, efficient and responsible our governmental processes. We must put the state's fiscal house in order. We must review—and revise—outmoded methods of the executive branch. We must erase all administrative abuses, all marks of waste and inefficiency, from our government. For only by such repairs and reforms can this government by the people be, seriously and literally, government for the people.

We must, wherever appropriate and proper for the state, effectively serve the needs of popular welfare. We must improve and expand the security provided in our programs of social insurance and health insurance. We must encourage urgently needed investment in private housing. We must do more and better work in the fields of physical and vocational rehabilitation. We must improve all our programs for the aged: health and recreation, housing and employment. With our rising standard of living and increasing leisure time it is important that the state give increasing encouragement to the intellectual and cultural facilities for the people. For—in all these areas of human want and need—government must have a heart as well as a brain.

We must truly strive to perfect the rule of our laws. We must promptly strengthen our whole court structure by thoughtful and thorough reorganization. We must—through the efficient mobilization of all enforcement officers and agencies—not only declare, but aggressively wage, war upon organized crime. And in all our laws and their enforcement we must and shall never forget the crime that is committed by any assault upon civil rights: here our vigor must match our vigilance. For it can be said of any state or nation: by their laws, you shall know them.

And we must work, perhaps hardest of all, on the field where the future can be won or lost: in our schoolrooms. We must attack the problems of juvenile delinquency. We must continue urgently needed state aid to our schools. We must plan—years into the future—expansion of our state institutions for higher education. For what we do not teach, we cannot save—and this is true of freedom itself.

In all such ways may we citizens of New York prove worthy of being citizens of the nation that is the best and strongest hope on earth for free men everywhere.

In such tasks, we can give little time or care to conventional labels or slogans. They have little meaning in terms of the realities of life today.

We shall be conservative—for we know the measureless value that is our heritage, to save and to cherish and to enrich.

We shall be liberal—for we are vastly more interested in the opportunities of tomorrow than the problems of yesterday.

We shall be progressive—for the opportunities and the challenges are of such size and scope that we can never halt and say: our labor is done.

Above all, we know the world we live in—and the values for which we strive.

We shall never surrender to the belief that man is a soulless device made to serve a machine or a state. We know that the state—and machines—are properly conceived and designed to serve man.

We shall never yield our faith in the spiritual nature of man: not a common creature of the same forces that rust iron and ripen corn—but a creature truly designed to serve his Maker and his own true good, his own full promise.

Let us unite in common cause—with hope and faith and love, with vision and courage. Together we can thus work toward the goal of freedom of opportunity for men everywhere in a world of peace.

I shall need your help and your trust.

I ask that help—and I pledge myself consistently to serve that trust.

EDUCATION

EDUCATION IN A TIME OF TESTING [1]

HARRY S. ASHMORE [2]

Harry S. Ashmore, editor of the *Arkansas Gazette,* Little Rock, gave this address at Washington University, St. Louis, on October 1, 1958. The speech reflected clearly Ashmore's thinking on the problem of integration and his philosophy concerning this problem and its relation to national progress.

Ashmore's reputation as a public speaker developed after his appointment in April 1947 as editor of the Charlotte (North Carolina) *News* and his address to the American Society of Newspaper Editors. In 1948 he gave a widely quoted speech to the Southern Political Science Association in which he dealt with segregation in the South and asserted that "the denial of civil rights that has always gone along with it has become indefensible." In 1951 he addressed the Governors' Conference in Arkansas. There he told the group that if integration of the races could not be forced by law, then neither could it be forbidden by law. In 1954, on the program of the Herald Tribune Freedom Forum, held at Hunter College, New York City, he explained the general problem of race relations in the South. In October 1958, he accepted an award at Freedom House, New York City.

Referred to by many southerners as "Public Enemy Number One," Ashmore nevertheless has described himself as a "moderate" concerned not so much "with the moral implications of segregation as with a common-sense, realistic approach."

His thesis in the Washington University speech was his quotation from Walter Prescott Webb, Texas historian: "Again history has passed . . . [the South] by, this time in reference to educational practice." To Ashmore, emotionality has affected decisions in Little Rock, as would be the case in many another American city. Democracy must have intellectually mature citizens if it is to function properly or even survive. His was a plea for educated philosophers as well as for technicians, "a sufficient number of kindred spirits to direct our practical affairs with a calm and insight that match their courage."

[1] Text supplied by Harry S. Ashmore, with permission for this reprinting. The speech was published in the February 1959 issue of the *Washington University Magazine* (Volume 28, Number 2).

[2] For biographical note, see Appendix.

Ashmore's style is direct, journalistic, lively, original. He speaks fluently. His voice is soft, easy to listen to and free from any noticeable southern accent. His eye contact is good, his body responsive to his ideas. He is a man of conviction and purpose. He reads or extemporizes, depending on the formality of the speaking situation. His television interviews are always extemporaneous.[3]

These days a man who bears my mailing address is expected to say something about Little Rock when he arises before any audience to speak on any subject.

So I should like to dispose of this obligation at the very beginning of these remarks. About the only thing I have to say about Little Rock today is that I don't plan to talk about it—at least not about the immediate moral, legal, and political issues that currently have their focus in my weary and battered home town.

Yet I have to concede that there is no way I can avoid Little Rock entirely and stay within the limits of the open-ended title for this address I submitted in a moment of panic when some efficient soul on the other end of a telephone reminded me that a program was about to go to the printers. "Education in a Time of Testing" does have a nice, resounding academic ring that seemed to me appropriate to the occasion—although, like you, I am not entirely certain what it means.

But this loose-leaf title does bring me back in a way to Little Rock—where education is certainly in a time of testing, and one that seems to have no end. We don't know whether we are going to have public high schools, or private high schools, or no high schools—and there was one dread moment when there was even some doubt that we would have football. This prospect, however, proved to be unthinkable, and the football teams have stayed in business even though the classrooms have been closed for a month. As John Lardner observed in *Newsweek,* Governor Faubus was able to cope with the left-wingers, but the single-wingers were too much for even that doughty man to bear.

[3] The information in this introduction is based partly on a graduate research study, "Harry Ashmore as Speaker," by Miss Mildred Lane, Department of Speech, State University of Iowa, 1958.

It is my own view that the great issue in Little Rock is not the education which our high school children are not now getting, or that which presumably they eventually will get on uncertain terms yet to be determined. The education that is really being put to the test is that to which all of the adults of the community have been subjected in the past—the schooling most of us obtained in the calm days when the Plessy Decision was undisputedly the law of the land, the Negro was safely in the place assigned to him by the white majority, and any knocking on the wall of segregation was a remote and muffled sound.

Those of us who had the benefit of public and/or private education in that quieter time when race relations were not an immediate issue are in charge of the situation in Little Rock—insofar as a mass of leaderless citizens are ever in charge of any public affair. We are the ones who went to the polls on last Saturday and voted by a margin of some three to one to keep our high schools closed unless we could have them opened on a segregated basis. The fact that the white people of the town preferred segregated schools was hardly a surprise; this was as safe an assumption as ever prompted any governor to run for a third term. The really significant thing was that a substantial number of us went merrily off to vote for something we knew in advance we could not have—a condition of which we were forcefully reminded by the United States Supreme Court before the glasses had been washed after the victory celebrations.

There were some who in their own terms were striking a blow for principle—speaking out for segregation without regard for the consequences, saying in effect that if they could not have unsegregated schools they would prefer to have none. It is possible to admire the courage and determination of these who, it may be assumed, had made a conscious decision to sacrifice for what they believed to be right. But I am convinced that those who voted in the spirit of the martyrs were a small minority. The great majority voted for the palpably false premise simply because they wanted to believe it was true; in the face of all the evidence to the contrary they accepted Governor Faubus's word that he would find a way to give them the same schools they had had before, without Negro students, and by lawful means. They were not persuaded to this view by the skill with which Mr. Faubus presented his case; they believed him simply because he was telling them what they wanted to hear.

This seems to me to be by far the most alarming aspect of the Little Rock story, which of course in microcosm is the southern story. The great moral, social, and constitutional questions that have come to focus on the issue of desegregation are of the first importance, and their resolution is urgent. But before there is any hope of resolution, the southern people—and indeed the American people—have got to reduce the issue to rational terms. To do this they must see the required transition in proper perspective—a view that will dim the hopes of some and soothe the fears of others. Walter Prescott Webb, the Texas historian, has stated the case simply and well in these words addressed to the Southern Historical Association, of which he is president:

> If the South in 1860 would have looked at the world, it would have seen that history had passed it by. Chattel slavery had been abolished almost throughout the Western world. The South was already but a tiny island of slavery in a rising sea of freedom of sorts. Its inundation was inevitable.
>
> Today the South finds itself in the same position. Again history has passed it by, this time in reference to educational practice. Nowhere else in the Western world, which is one community, with the exception of parts of Africa, is there such discrimination as the South has used and continues to use in many places. Again it is an island in a rising sea, and its inundation is again spoken, and, like it or not, the South must eventually accept the decision, however deliberate its speed. The South tried to escape the inevitable once, and has suffered for it ever since. It cannot afford to make the same mistake twice. It cannot afford to be diverted by a cause already lost.

The fact that Professor Webb and I agree that this is a fair rendering of the reality before the South does not, of course, make it so. It should, however, at least make the proposition a fit subject for rational debate among all those concerned with the southern problem. But the appalling truth is that so far the proposition has been rejected out of hand by the southern leadership, public and privâte, and the man who even states it is subject to some peril.

There is a comfortable assumption around the country that this reaction is the product of an affliction peculiar to southerners —that the tenuous grip on reality which has characterized most of my fellow-citizens recently is unique to Arkansans and their near neighbors. As a part of this thesis, it is presumed, by people far removed from the reality of Little Rock, that the people of the South are a backward breed of inferior social standards and primitive customs who have been denied access to the superior educational facilities available elsewhere in the country. I will not here debate the validity of the measurements by which professional educators determine the comparative excellence of public school systems. I will, indeed, stipulate that my state has known much poverty and consequently has suffered from much ignorance. But we are not talking about rural Arkansas, but urban Little Rock—and Little Rock is a pleasant, prosperous and reasonably sophisticated community which would compare favorably with almost any city of its size I have known in this country or abroad. There are a certain number of citizens of demonstrably inferior education in the large company that seems disposed to follow the lemmings over the edge of this particular cliff of history—but there are also those who are the product of a first-rate public school system, and of eastern universities respectably coated with ivy.

I do not belabor these points in an effort to inspire your compassion for a people in their time of trouble and sorrow. Rather I invite you to consider the frightening possibility that the people of Little Rock are not unique, but very well may be typical of Americans in the middle of this critical century. No others of our people have been subjected to quite the same emotional tensions that are produced by the conflict between the new racial requirements of the United States Supreme Court and the established customs and mores of a Confederate state. But if we assume that in different terms a comparable situation could arise in Cedar Rapids, or Fresno, or Providence, or here in St. Louis, are we justified in assuming that the citizenry would react more rationally and with greater restraint?

On the basis of the record of my time, I have my doubts. Indeed, it seems to me far more understandable that a majority of the confused, bewildered, and frightened citizens of Arkansas should accept the dubious propositions set forth by Governor Faubus than that a comparable majority of the people of the United States should have elected in 1952 a President who had no known position on any of the pressing issues of the day and in effect candidly disclaimed any responsibility for the policies of the political party which had nominated him. Here too was a mass emotional reaction; we were weary of trouble and hard decisions and were willing to settle for an unsupported promise of peace—which was different in context but not in kind from that held out by Orval Faubus.

There are many other tests we might apply, with equally dismaying results, to determine whether the educational system we have built and cherished in our country is really producing in sufficient quantity those open-minded, informed, and intellectually mature citizens we have always assumed a democracy must have if it is to function properly, or even to survive. One obvious and timely matter is the inability of this country, to date at least, to stage a rational and constructive public debate on an issue upon which the fate of the world may currently turn—diplomatic recognition of Red China. Even with artillery batteries engaged daily across the narrow strait that separates Nationalist Quemoy and the Communist mainland, and sending a shiver through every chancellery in the world each time a lanyard is pulled, the vast majority of our elected officials still do not consider it prudent to bring up the subject of dealing with the *de facto* government of China on any more realistic a basis than a discussion between low-ranking ambassadors in Warsaw. The reason, of course, is that we are still suffering the aftereffects of a national fever that was almost as debilitating as that produced by desegregation in the South—the strange seizure of McCarthyism which produced a climate in which any loyal American who suggested that it might be possible to do business with a Communist government opened himself to the charge of treason. I have no way of knowing the extent of the hazard involved in negotiations with the Reds, whether they be Russian or Chinese. But I am convinced that the peril is less than that inherent in a climate of opinion in which it is an act of political courage to suggest that the only way to find out is to try.

All of which seems to me to say a good deal about American public education, most of it unfavorable. It is proper that we worry about whether Johnny can spell—or perhaps more urgently whether Johnny can count past ten with his shoes on—since the latest wave of public, or at least public relations, concern over education was produced by the realization that the Russian mechanics make a better Sputnik than ours do. But it is far more important that Johnny understand the world he lives in and be endowed with the courage and the will to come to grips with it—qualities with which our system of education does not seem to have conspicuously endowed Johnny's father.

There even seems to be a danger that this essential aspect of education may suffer still more as a result of the new public concern over the presumed failure of our educational system to turn out enough technicians. It is, of course, a happy thing if a state legislature steps up its appropriations for the schools and colleges because it has discovered that we are running short of high school physics teachers, while the Russian *Gymnasia* are adequately and even abundantly supplied. But somehow I can't imagine a legislature becoming exercised because we are also running short of philosophers—who still seem to me to be essential, although admittedly they are not the object of campus raids by the representatives of private industry.

I suggest that the concenetration on technical education, essential though it is, in itself can be, and all too often has been, an escape from reality. Of course we need men who can split atoms, build dams, cure cancer, and meet payrolls—and I have no objection if these receive the greatest material rewards of our abundant society. But we also need men who can teach us to live together without blowing each other up—men who figure that the human body is hardly worth pampering or even salvaging if its only use is to house a sterile spirit. No one is going to find the solution to this essential problem in the quiet and order of the laboratory. Such a pursuit requires a chilling plunge into the uncertainties of our contemporary society, and a disposition to challenge the standards we live by. And it quite likely will lead to unpopularity—a condition that seems to be becoming increasingly intolerable in this age of togetherness when the highest aim of man is to be universally loved, or, failing that, ignored.

Perhaps the only certainty before any of us today is that we are going to live for the foreseeable future in a state of flux. The concepts upon which this republic was founded are still valid and must be preserved—but their very preservation requires that we recognize that they must be applied today to a society almost totally different from that in which they were conceived. We are not now, and have not been for decades, a people who live on the land or in small towns or manageable cities. The physical surroundings that once gave us a sense of tranquillity and afforded time for reflection are gone; the husbandman and the independent artisan upon whose basic wisdom Jefferson relied for stability in democratic society are no longer with us—or are so few in number as to be a minor influence. We are, for the most part, an urban people caught up in a grinding industrial society that has created a new problem for every one it has solved—and we are rapidly becoming a rootless people shorn of those traditional ties to place and family that once characterized the mass of Americans and gave us our essential values. Materially, we are, of course, better off than we have ever been—but we are pretty far along in a process that bids fair to replace poverty of person with poverty of the soul.

I can offer no certain cure for the condition in which we find ourselves. But I can suggest that some of the developments that inspire optimism among our public orators not only hold out no hope of salvation but, by distracting us from the hard, lonely consideration of the nature of our ailment, often do positive harm. I am, for example, wholly unimpressed by the figures that show that more of us are going to church than ever before. What is important is what happens to us after we get inside a church—and I entertain serious doubt that anything useful happens to the member of a congregation that has been substantially increased by the installation of a bowling alley in the church basement.

So it is with the schools. It is a wonderful statistic that proves that we virtually have no illiterates in this country now—on paper the fruition of a dream for which generations have made real sacrifices. But the statistic means practically nothing if the only test is the ability to read and write and do ciphers. Literacy in any meaningful sense must imply a familiarity with great writing and great ideas—and a disposition to continue the search for truth wherever it may lead. I do not, unhappily, often find any correlation between literacy in this dimension and the years a person has gone to school, or even the degrees he holds.

As I have said, the highest purpose of education is to equip Johnny to come to grips with the reality of the time he lives in. And it is in this sense that I charge that education at all levels is failing in this time of testing. We have always been afflicted by those H. G. Wells has called the Godsakers—those who wring their hands and cry, "For God's sake, somebody do something," every time something goes wrong with the affairs of man, which we must accept now as a permanent condition. These might be called Godsakers of the Left, but there are also Godsakers of the Right—those who cry, "For God's sake, let's don't change anything," no matter how clear the evidence that the future has overwhelmed the past. In either case it doesn't take much to send a Godsaker over the line and into the company of those Eric Hoffer has described as the True Believers. Once someone devises a cause that is somehow tailored to his own fears and delusions the True Believer becomes an active crusader—operating, as Hoffer says, within a fact-proof screen and following his leader without regard to personal hazard or even rational belief that his goal can be attained. The True Believers constitute a powerful force, for good or for evil. They gave the motive power to Christianity in the days of the martyrs. But they also made Adolf Hitler possible, and they form the marching bands of the world-wide Communist crusade that we deem to be our greatest peril. Let it be sadly noted that our system of universal free education, by all the tests I have mentioned, does not seem to have materially reduced the proportion of active or incipient True Believers in our own society.

Perhaps this could never be done, even if the schools and colleges were as good as I hope they one day will be. Maybe the reality of our time is so unpleasant that only the hardiest among us have the spiritual resources to maintain more than a tenuous grip upon it. But if this is so, then our institutions of learning have an even greater obligation to serve this hardier breed and increase its numbers if they can—to provide a spiritual home for the unbemused man of clear sight and inquiring mind, and send out into the world a sufficient number of kindred spirits to direct our practical affairs with a calm and insight that match their courage.

We must assume that mankind, even in a society as free as ours, will continue to run in a herd when panic whitens the eye and shakes the hand. Where man runs, then, will depend upon how he is led—and the quality of his leadership will be the ultimate test of our system of education.

PRESENT-DAY AMERICAN LIFE: ITS ORDER OF VALUES, AND ITS SENSE OF DIRECTION [4]

J. WILLIAM FULBRIGHT [5]

Senator J. William Fulbright of Arkansas delivered this speech before the United States Senate on August 21, 1958. In the closing hours of the Eighty-fifth Congress, second session, the Senator gave his general philosophy of the state of the nation and an analysis of American attitudes, values, purposes, and sense of direction.

This was one of the most statesmanlike speeches delivered in the United States Senate in the past fifty years. It was concise in its analysis of the attitudes of the American people. Its indictment of a whole people was developed without partisan or political bias. The language was also original. The former training of the Senator, including his studies as a Rhodes scholar, and his experience as governor of his state as well as his leadership in the Senate in educational legislation, was apparent on this speaking occasion. As usual, his delivery was animated, clear cut, and audience-dominating.

At the conclusion of his speech Fulbright was lauded by Senator Mike Mansfield of Montana and Senator Prescott Bush of Connecticut. Senator Alexander Wiley of Wisconsin praised the speech but argued that neither the President nor Congress could be blamed for events or circumstances outside the United States and beyond our control. Senator Stuart Symington of Missouri endorsed Fulbright's remarks on the deficiencies in American education as compared with Soviet efforts, and Senator Frank Lausche of Ohio took note of Fulbright's fearlessness in stressing points that might bring adverse comment.[6]

It is part of our litany in public life to say that the people speak with the voice of God. I do not question that. Much less do I question the institutions and practices of democracy that draw their vitality from that principle. But I would feel myself a toadying sycophant if I didn't speak one plain truth. It is that the people, for some years now, have spoken with the voice of a false God—and it is a voice which has impressed itself

[4] From a text furnished by Senator Fulbright. Text published in the *Congressional Record.* 104:17412-18 (daily edition). August 21, 1958.

[5] For biographical note, see Appendix.

[6] For further comment on Fulbright as a speaker see the Cumulative Author Index for references to his speeches in earlier volumes.

on what government itself has been doing during this period. If things have gone wrong, the people are not without blame in the matter.

The last thing that can be said about our foreign policy in the last few years is that it wasn't what the people wanted. Of course they wanted it! And what they got was exactly what they wanted—a foreign policy on the cheap, featuring a pact here, and a shipment of a few guns there.

The people wanted to believe that after years of cold-war strain, they were at liberty to stop thinking any more. They wanted to believe that after years of cold-war sacrifice, they could bask in the artificial sunlight of a government which did not bother them with serious things. They wanted to believe that in a world full of menace, the way to get out of the line of danger was to have a government which used such energy as it had to the end that everything should stand still. And if things somehow refused to stand still, then the thing to do was to lasso what was in motion by tossing out another attitude, another platitude, another beatitude.

Can anyone in this chamber deny this? Can anyone here deny that the distinguishing feature of American society during much of the decade of the 1950's was its weakness for the easy way? Can anyone deny that in this period, we were the opposite of what our Founding Fathers had in mind for the new America?

The Founding Fathers said—and here I quote from the first paragraph of the *Federalist* papers—they said:

> It seems to have been reserved to the people of this country, by their conduct and example, to decide the important question, whether societies of men are really capable of establishing good government from reflection and choice, or whether they are forever destined to depend for their constitutions on accident and force.

But I ask you now: What show of "reflection and choice" was there in much of the decade of the 1950's when the word "egghead" became a word of abuse; when education was neglected; when intellectual excellence became a cause for suspicion; when the man in public life, or the writer, or the teacher, who dared articulate an original thought risked being accused of subversion. What show of "reflection and choice" was there in this period when the man of distinction was the man who had a station wagon, a second car plated with chrome, a swimming pool, a tax-free expense account, and a twenty-one-inch color television set with the thirty-six-inch star on its screen?

It was precisely because there was so little reflection and choice in this period, that what we got in our government was a government which entrusted the highest interests of state to the play of accident and force. For whenever we brought ourselves to do anything at all about a crisis that exploded before our astonished eyes, we almost automatically reached for bigger bombs and bigger bombers.

Mr. President, I am not opposed to bombers. But neither do I want SAC to become a nuclear version of the Maginot line. Yet that is what it is likely to become if the only thing we can think to do after each crisis, is to order some more arms—and then go to sleep on the arms. And that is what SAC is tending to become when after every crisis, our highest officers of state, without regard to their own responsibilities to speak plain truths, tell the people that the crisis was really just the passing shadow of a mirage—knowing that that is what the people want to think.

A frightening historical parallel has occurred to me with increasing frequency in recent weeks. Fifteen or sixteen centuries ago, the Roman empire was all-powerful, rich, successful—and also complacent. Neither the Roman emperors nor the Roman Senate could bring themselves to be overly concerned with the crude and boorish people to the north. Emperors were judged by the public entertainment they arranged, and the wealth and substance of the empire were dissipated in lavish consumption. When anyone was so inconsiderate as to call attention to the gathering clouds on the horizon, he was denounced as a prophet of gloom and doom and purged for un-Roman activity. In 1958, the critic is charged with "selling America short"!

This picture is admittedly oversimplified. But in broad outline it is pertinent and valid. The fall of great civilizations runs a well-defined course. On the outside, the civilization has a hard, shining surface, full of glitter and superficial accomplishment. But inside the outer shell, invisible decay does its work. And the hard shell collapses on the empty center when that civilization collides with a challenge it no longer has the power to meet, because it was indifferent to the challenge too long.

I do not believe that we Americans are incapable of meeting the challenge of the Soviet Union and of the nationalistic revolution going on in Asia and Africa. But I say in all seriousness that we do not have much time left in which to shed our indifference and do something about it. . . .

Until we do revise our sense of values, we will never think we can afford to do the things which, in my judgment, we must do if we are to survive as a free nation.

Is it not ridiculous, Mr. President, that we place a higher economic value on driving a truck than on teaching school?

Is it not out of all proportion that we accord greater social prestige to a rock 'n' roll singer than to a philosopher?

We are constantly told we cannot afford a good public school system, but we could have a very good one if we diverted to education even a fraction of what we spend on all manner of amusement and luxury. The only logical inference to be drawn from this fact is that we, as a people, would rather have the luxuries than the schools. Now, surely, Mr. President, this is getting things upside down. We are treating luxuries as necessities, and necessities as luxuries. And the irony of it is that we are not really confronted with this kind of choice. We are rich enough to have our cake and eat it too. But we have become so greedy, we want it à la mode.

So, Mr. President, I say we have got to revise our scale of values. We have got to return to a reasonable sense of what is really important, as distinguished from what is merely desirable. Fundamental to this process is a change in public attitudes toward public figures. We hear a great deal in the Senate, Mr. President, about our heavy responsibilities as senators and about the grave importance of the decisions which we make. This is all true. But I dare say there is not a member of this body who hasn't heard the word "politician" used as an epithet. I dare say that there are few members of this body who don't envy the happier standing that Mickey Mantle or Bob Hope enjoys in the nation.

I am not being critical of Mr. Mantle, who is an estimable young man and who performs valuable services for his employers.

I am simply saying that something has got to be done to bring things back into proper perspective. Some way must be found to increase public understanding of public affairs, and to develop a sense of values appropriate to the problems and decisions which confront our people.

I am frank to admit that I have no quick or easy solution to offer. There may be no solution at all. But if there is, it lies, I think, in long-term efforts in the field of education and not in superficial public relations campaigns masterminded from Madison Avenue.

Yet one of the most discouraging events of this session of Congress has been its action in regard to education. When Sputnik made it dazzlingly clear that we were falling behind the Russians in at least some fields of technology, our reaction was to pass an education bill designed to take a few feeble steps towards producing more scientists and improving the teaching of languages. Now, Heaven knows this needs to be done. I voted for it. But I suggest this is another instance in which our priorities are somewhat askew.

As badly as we need scientists and linguists, we even more badly need people who are capable of evaluating the work of the scientists and of making the enormously complicated decisions —which are essentially political decisions—that are called for if we are to adjust our policies and our life to our scientific progress. The age of the amateur is over. We can no longer look to our household experiences, or to "common-sense" knowledge if we are to pass good judgments on the new kind of life-and-death political-scientific questions which have become the leading questions of modern government. In addition to common sense, we need exact knowledge, which we can come by only through hard study shared in by everyone. In short, we need to become a nation of statesmen-scientists—just as much as we need atomic scientists. Unless we become a nation of statesmen-scientists, we can kiss good-bye to our whole traditional constitutional system for responsible power. It will be done for, because only a handful of experts will make decisions for the rest of us, and we will have no exact basis for knowing whether they decided well. . . .

We have gone through periods like this before in our national history, Mr. President. The decades of the 1920's and of the 1870's come readily to mind. In each case, we eventually came to our senses, went to work, and corrected a good deal of what had been wrong. Our situation is now more serious because the threat is more dangerous. Although we can take some comfort from history, we make a tragic—perhaps a fatal—mistake if we assume the inevitability of American national survival.

It is time, Mr. President, to cease going along as usual. It is time to test the slogans and the shibboleths by which we have lived this past decade, both in our relations with others and with ourselves. It is time to test them in the fires of free and honest discussion. Perhaps then, Mr. President, we shall get an answer to what is wrong in our foreign policy. Even more important, perhaps, we shall get an answer to what is wrong in our own national house.

I am not entirely without hope that this can be done. There are some signs that the American people are rousing themselves from the luxurious torpor which has afflicted them in recent years. All I can say is that it is high time. We have already turned off the alarm several times, and reset it for a later hour. We dare not do that again.

THE UNRECORDED LEGACY [7]

LESTER THONSSEN [8]

Dr. Lester Thonssen gave this address at the seventy-fifth annual Huron College commencement, on May 26, 1958, in the College Auditorium, Huron, South Dakota. During the program he was awarded the honorary degree of Doctor of Literature.

Dr. Thonssen was an undergraduate debater at Huron. He received his M.A. and Ph.D. degrees in speech at the State University of Iowa. Since 1931 he has been a member of the speech department at the City College of New York, and has served as visiting professor of speech at summer sessions at the universities of Montana, Iowa, Colorado, Southern California, and Hawaii, and at Teachers College, Columbia University. He has been editor of *Speech Monographs,* and was president of the Speech Association of America in 1956.

Dr. Thonssen is deeply grounded in classical rhetoric and the later rhetorical developments. His teaching methods and his own communicative practices reflect his background in such philosophy. In his public discourse as well as in his writings he upholds the primacy of logic and reason. His speeches are models of well-knit organization and arrangement, with an Attic style—perspicuous, adaptable, restrained, yet sufficiently imaginative and emotional to evoke effective audience response—and with delivery that is direct, vigorous, and markedly communicative.

In his essay on "The Anthropology of Manners," Edward T. Hall, Jr., tells of a tribesman who came to a prearranged spot in Kabul, the capital of Afghanistan, to meet his brother. But he couldn't find him. So he left, giving instructions to the local merchants where he might be reached if his brother showed up. Exactly a year later, the tribesman returned to the same place in Kabul, and sure enough, there was his brother. It seems that the brothers had agreed to meet in Kabul on a certain day of a certain month at a particular place, but they had failed to specify the year.

My plans have been like those of the tribesman. Often I've agreed to meet friends on a return to the campus at commencement time, but the year was never definitely set. Now, thirty-two

[7] Text supplied through the courtesy of Dr. Lester Thonssen, with permission for this reprint.

[8] For biographical note, see Appendix.

years after graduation—a disturbingly grim statistic—I'm honored and privileged to keep an appointment on this important occasion in the life of a fine institution.

To President Kerr and his faculty, I'm grateful for the invitation to take part in the commencement program. No words of thanks, however happily expressed, can convey my warm appreciation of this honor. It's a deep satisfaction to come home to Huron College.

My remarks tonight will be addressed both to an institution and its students.

This is a birthday. Not just a routine birthday, but a very special one. It marks three quarters of a century of service in the enterprise of humane learning. This is a reminder of our debt to men and women of vision, or if you prefer, of dreams. Less than two decades after the first permanent settlement was made in this area, and six years before South Dakota was admitted to statehood, dedicated pioneers recognized the need for disciplined learning. They gave of their considerable skills; they shaped a vision into a reality. We are the beneficiaries.

Today is more than an anniversary, however. It's a time of high excitement in the lives of the favored young men and women who make up the graduating class. They give full meaning to this moment, for they constitute the only reason for an institution's existence. Through them alone can the past of this college, with its accumulations of wisdom and practical experience, find a voice in the present.

Much of what we commemorate today deals, of course, with the past. Seventy-five years of leadership by the college are completed, and you—the members of the graduating class—have finished the baccalaureate course. What, then, can I say that will link the past with the present? Perhaps very little, if anything, that's new. I'll deal largely in reminiscences and reflections on liberal education. And, unlike many commencement speakers, I'll go lightly on advice. I'll take counsel from the story of the boy who was asked on an examination, "Who was Socrates?" His answer was short and neat. "Socrates was a Greek. He went around giving people advice. The people poisoned Socrates."

Moreover, I'll offer little prophecy or prediction. I don't pretend to know how to read the future.

I begin with four basic assumptions.

In the first place, education, however good, will not guarantee a perfect world. As Mark Van Doren once put it: "Education does not pose as insurance against error and sin. There will continue to be plenty of both in a universe which man did not create, and which he inhabits as a more or less refractory citizen." Furthermore, the most gifted teachers can't guarantee that their students will all turn out well. Some pupils of the greatest teachers in history turned out to be scoundrels. Judas Iscariot betrayed Jesus; although taught by the illustrious Socrates, Alcibiades became a villain of the deepest hue; Nero had his teacher, Seneca, executed.

Secondly, no institution is ever wholly satisfied with the education it gives its students. It's clearly impossible to fill every staff position at the highest level of competence. Nor is it possible, within the limits of budgets, to provide the optimum in laboratories and work facilities. Since the ideal curriculum is in heaven, one shouldn't expect to find it on earth. This is true whether the number of course offerings is large or small. An official at the University of Chicago is reported to have said that the depression of the 1930's was the best thing to happen to the program there during his experience, for it resulted in the abolition of about four hundred courses, to the great benefit of the educational system.

The third assumption is that no student is ever completely satisfied with the education he gets. He feels that he was required to take courses he didn't need, was offered Hobson's choices among equally distasteful "free electives," had no opportunity at all to take others he wanted, met up with teachers who contributed little to the abundant life, and was a victim of some teaching practices that were worthless, or even downright harmful. The more cynical students may even say that they would have turned out just as well without any formal courses. This brings to mind a passage from the 1954 Report of the President of the Rockefeller Foundation. The question was asked: "What do the [Rockefeller] fellowships produce?" One official answered "that if the Foundation should follow the same careful selection procedure and, instead of awarding a fellowship, should tattoo a mark on the man selected, he would rise to high level of attainment without the fellowship." To which an eminent scientist, a former recipient of a fellowship, replied: "Perhaps, but I'm glad I got a fellowship and not a tattoo mark!"

My fourth assumption is also common knowledge. Much of what the student learned from books will be forgotten, some of it promptly, much of it irrecoverably. We who teach may hesitate to admit this, but that won't alter the fact. Perhaps we may take heart from the suspicion that some of what is forgotten may not be worth remembering anyway.

These assumptions have a negative import, but they help us put positive details in sharper focus. Let's consider, then, certain ways in which a college education contributes to the lives of the students. And as we proceed, let's mention some recent developments which endanger the full realization of these objectives.

Samuel Johnson once remarked that "curiosity is one of the permanent and certain characteristics of a vigorous intellect." In short, the cultivated mind is inquisitive. It's eager to engage in the unending search for truth. This brings me to the first of the positive contributions which college training affords the student. The college experience should stimulate a lively spirit of inquiry.

Recent world events have sparked an uncommon interest in our educational system. Criticisms and recommendations have been offered freely in the interest of insuring our leadership in a technological age. Obviously, educators welcome the suggestions. But we must weigh certain of the proposals very carefully. Otherwise we'll find ourselves giving assent to the erroneous conclusion that training in the liberal arts is a luxury, and the equally dubious conclusion that the educational process can be carried out under conditions of haste and speed.

Doubtless much time is wasted in our present set-up. Many gifted students are probably held back by the slow pace set by the less able. These shortcomings should be dealt with. But I have misgivings about proposals which contain even the faintest hint that the training of a person can be accomplished quickly. My misgivings stem from the fear that, while making haste, we inadvertently or otherwise make the training program easy, or bypass the necessities of extensive reading, sustained reflection, and unhurried exploration in the realm of ideas. The spirit of inquiry cannot but suffer under such restriction.

In one of his dialogues, Plato remarks:

> There is a saying of wiser men than ourselves that a man of sense should not try to please his fellow-servants . . . but his good and noble masters, so that, if the way is long and circuitous, marvel not at this; for, where the end is great, there the way may be permitted to be long. . . .

In the *Republic,* Plato also speaks of a guardian's not growing faint in search of truth; he must be willing to take the longer road. And again from the dialogue:

> Anyone who cares about seed, and wants it to grow into a crop, will not plant a "garden of Adonis" and be pleased when it shoots up in eight days, but will prefer proper agriculture, and be glad when the seed finally bears fruit after eight months of laborious care.

This concept from Plato is referred to as "the long detour."

Plato was largely concerned at the time with a program of philosophical training for the orator. But the principle is equally applicable to the total process of education.

I know of no formula for the easy, swift training of a mind. Before a student, however intelligent, can roam in the field of ideas, and explore and pursue inquiries, he must have grounding in the arts and disciplines of his calling. The late Hoyt Hudson, one of Huron College's most distinguished sons, remarked that there "are three foes against which liberal education—or the educated person—must fight unremitting warfare. . . ." He called them "ignorance, muddleheadedness, and crassness," or in other words, "lack of information, lack of operative logic, and lack of imagination." Surely no one would believe that a person comes by a well-rounded body of facts, skill in their handling and expression, and sensitivity to their implications in a quick, easy way. He must be prepared to take "the long detour." No one should exepect to ride to an education over a high-speed turnpike.

The temper of our time is clearly one of haste. But ordinarily, a spirited sense of inquiry doesn't flourish properly in a hurried climate. There must be time to acquire information, time to reflect, time to explore, time to discover, time to develop skills. In an emergency, a man, like an engine, can do astounding feats under forced draft. But in the long run—and education doesn't follow any other course—time is a powerful ally. The human mind isn't a jug into which information can be poured like so many doses of a medical prescription. Science hasn't yet come up with a miracle drug for the swift removal of ignorance.

Let's turn to a second area in which a college contributes to its students. I submit that it should develop a genuine hospitality of mind for talk.

Ours is a verbal society. We're surrounded by words. The number of words uttered—should you have a bent for statistical detail—is of an astronomical order. Stuart Chase combined various assumptions as to the number of talking people, the length of time each spoke daily, and came up with a total of about twelve trillion, or four quadrillion words a year. So of one thing we can be sure. There is much talk, some good, some bad.

A college has an obligation to cultivate in students a wholesome point of view toward talk. Among the first essentials is the cultivation of a willingness to listen to it, for there is much cynicism about the efficacy of talk. Everyone knows men and women who have little confidence in what anyone says. Moreover, many people are plainly allergic to words, other than their own. Words have a toxic effect on them. Like the hayfever sufferer who breaks out on exposure to ragweed, these people break out in a rash of squirms and twitchings on exposure to talk.

To create an abiding respect for talk is a stern assignment. It means an institution must hold its students to rigorous standards of thought. It's an unending job of creating conditions that will help train people to think.

If a college provides proper training and opportunities for practice, surely it has a right to expect its graduates to be able to make severe analyses of complex social problems, know the difference between opinions and facts, have a respect for evidence, be willing to follow facts to their logical conclusions, and express their conclusions with dignity and intellectual precision.

A wholesome point of view toward talk doesn't mean acceptance of everything one hears, whether it's from this platform, the community forum, the Senate of the United States, or the Security Council of the United Nations. A man has an inalienable right to dislike a statement. That's a healthy, democratic prerogative. What's necessary, however, is an attitude favorably receptive to *entertain* the ideas. What we need are persons who'll receive talk as they do visitors, and then judge both on their merits.

Our democratic heritage makes us proud of the tradition of honest dissent. But this tradition has been buffeted about in recent years. Some persons have drawn little distinction between honest dissent and disloyalty. Criticism has become suspect, even though it's essential to the correction of evils.

Certain pressures toward conformity of view have been persistent and intense. This has affected the public attitude toward controversy and difference of opinion. Dissident ideas have become objects of fear, with the result that the range of expression has seemingly been narrowed. This is a matter of deep concern to educators.

Doubtless the defender of unpopular views fares less well in our classes today than he did twenty-five years ago. He's more likely to be singled out as an intellectual eccentric. The patterns of conformity make the going harder for him, and more dangerous. He may pay, in terms of future employment, for his youthful expression of views which at the moment are unpopular. So certain matters are discussed fearfully, or not at all. The discussion process is accordingly used at reduced efficiency.

Judge Learned Hand underscored the general problem with these wise remarks:

> I believe that that community is already in process of dissolution where each man begins to eye his neighbor as a possible enemy, where nonconformity with the accepted creed, political as well as religious, is a mark of disaffection; where denunciation, without specification or backing, takes the place of evidence; where orthodoxy chokes freedom of dissent; where faith in the eventual supremacy of reason has become so timid that we dare not enter our convictions in the open lists to win or lose.

I'd say then, ladies and gentlemen, that a college must provide an atmosphere congenial to talk. Regardless of our occupation or profession, we'll all spend a sizable part of our lives making and remaking adjustments to a linguistic environment. The least we, as educators, can do is to cultivate in our students a willingness to listen, sharpen their intellectual faculties in the use of tools of thought and expression, and provide a wholesome respect for diversity of opinion.

I believe it was Dr. Tavares, a Brazilian writer, who said Americans treated lecturers with uncommon kindness. American audiences, so he said, will put up with anything, provided they know how long it's going to last. Let me comfort you by saying that I now come to my final thesis.

I submit that the college should cultivate in students an appreciation of the Golden Mean in thought and action. This isn't a plea for conservatism of view. Nor does it imply that college students should be rubber stamps, automatically endorsing old patterns of thought and fearing to initiate bold, new ideas. Most emphatically, quite the contrary. What I do say, however, is that the educated man or woman should have a sense of measure, of proportion. In short, he should have good judgment. He should be able to sense the fine balance between sufficiency and excess. This notion of the Mean was dear to the mind of the ancient Greeks. They saw in it a sort of philosophical measure of the ideal life—a life in which wisdom prevailed. There should be neither too much nor too little, neither excess nor deficiency. Right reason should prescribe the proper amounts.

In one of his major works, Aristotle makes light of someone's question whether the narrative part of a composition should be developed quickly or slowly. Remarked Aristotle: "I would say, as did one to a baker, who inquired 'whether he should knead his bread hard or soft,' 'What,' said he, 'is it then impossible to knead it properly?' " In other words, there should be a Mean: neither too much nor too little, neither too many nor too few of whatever parts make up the whole.

The college experience should help students achieve a balance between spur and bridle, between energy and moderation. Let me mention two ways in which it can.

An institution should, through example, teach its students that there's a fine balance between dedicated service and indoctrination. Many of the teachers at Huron College have through the years expressed this principle with extraordinary effect. Without offense to the others who deserve mention, I bring to mind a few I knew, although I didn't have classes under all of them. Elisabeth Reid, Louise French, William Notestein, Ella McIntire, Miriam Crawford Speirs. One would indeed be insensitive to selfless devotion if he didn't respond warmly to such names. They brought a gentleness and dignity to learning. They did what Guy Stanton Ford considered the secret of the great teacher: each engaged "his students with him in a joint enterprise of equal importance to both." They didn't find it necessary to engage in a selling campaign to bring us to an appreciation of the joy of learning; they knew when to apply the spur, when to use the bridle.

They loved their subjects, as all good teachers must. But they transmitted a contagious enthusiasm not only for *their* subjects, but for other disciplines as well. They did it, moreover, without immoderate pleadings, without sectarian or partisan slants, without pedagogical hocus-pocus. They knew what some educators today seem reluctant to admit, namely, that a subject may be valuable even though it isn't as interesting or appealing as another subject. Subjects of worth require effort. And hard work adds excitement to learning. Sugar-coating subjects to reduce effort, or to heighten their palatability, may very well render them less useful. Granted a willingness on the part of students to learn, it shouldn't be necessary to teach basic subjects under soft lights, with sweet music, and with intermittent movies for diversionary relief. It shouldn't be necessary to underscore an important principle or concept by releasing a flock of pigeons, or by sending up a Roman candle. No one will deny that that would make education interesting, in the worst sense of the word. Classrooms should not be devoted to the cultivation of an easy mediocrity.

In an age in which sentiment is mildly suspect, it may yet be well to recall that men and women of deep faith in the power of learning sustained this institution, and that without pleading special causes, or relying on academic gadgetry, furnished the information and skills which young minds need to acquire intellectual competence.

I'll mention but one other way in which the college should help the student in the cultivation of a Golden Mean in personal conduct.

Although it's less evident here than in many parts of America, our society is being urbanized. Accordingly, it's becoming increasingly difficult for large segments of the population to strike a reasonable balance between the world of nature and the world man has built upon the land. Perhaps many people no longer care whether they establish that balance. If true, so much greater the tragedy.

This is a land of incredible natural beauty. But one can't travel far without coming squarely upon a shocking conclusion. In our frenetic rush to use the land and its plant and animal resources, we're giving preciously little attention simply to enjoying it. This state of mind is pervasive. It seems that we no longer have much interest or desire to enjoy the natural resources for their beauty. The names of natural wonders cast few magical spells. To many nowadays, a mayflower is more likely to be associated with a brand of coffee or a moving company, than with the plant of the field. I can believe the story that a tourist, looking into the Grand Canyon, asked whether it was a WPA project. And I surely can believe the report of a friend of mine who, on completing a transcontinental auto trip, said he didn't see much along the way. To begin with, he wasn't interested in seeing much. And if he ever did want to look at a hillside of flowers or a stand of young trees, his view was probably obstructed by some tawdry sign proclaiming the medicinal triumph of a new foot powder, or picturing the ingredients of the world's longest homogenized hotdog. It's no longer easy to capture the spirit of the land by driving through it.

And to suggest that anyone take a long walk in the fields and woods is almost heresy. It used to be fun to walk to school, even for distances of two or three miles. Nowadays if a youngster has to walk three hundred yards to the highway to board his school bus, he thinks he's being victimized.

As for many of the tourists who decide to walk into the less accessible areas of beauty in our parks and monuments, the act of using their legs hasn't heightened their sense of responsibility. Through some primitive compulsion many are obliged to carve their initials on the most stately trees, and wantonly pull up the wild flowers which evidently obstruct free passage to the lake or whatever the point of beauty is at the end of the trail. At the destination, those insensitive to visual delights throw a few stones at the birds in the nearest tree, then retrace their steps back over the trail, and soon report to their friends that the trip wasn't worth the effort.

You may be asking yourself: What has this to do with the immediate theme? Very much indeed. An educated man should combine a love of what is useful with what is beautiful. The college has a responsibility to provide training and foster attitudes that will orient students properly to the biotic community of which they're members. This means more than giving a course in nature study, important as that may be. It involves building up a complex set of attitudes, underlining man's interdependence upon land, water, animals, and plants.

The cultivated mind must strike an alliance between the natural world—or at least such parts of it as man hasn't yet destroyed—and the world of bricks and stones and dams and other useful paraphernalia we call modern society. If his love for the useful is tempered by his love and respect for the natural, he'll respond with greater sensitivity to the splendor of a sunset, the opening of a spring flower, the graceful sweep of a hawk in flight, the magical tapestry of a field of ripening wheat. There's still room for a bit of poetry in men's lives. "We must live for something besides making a living," said Joseph Wood Krutch. And he added: "If we do not permit the earth to produce beauty and joy, it will in the end not produce food either."

These, then, my friends of the graduating class, are certain of the objectives of a college education: the stimulation of a lively curiosity for the truth, the development of a hospitality of mind for talk, and the cultivation of a Golden Mean in personal conduct. Because I have a deep faith in this institution, I'm sure that these aims have been substantially achieved. Accordingly, I would count these gains as parts of the unrecorded legacy which this college passes on to you. They do not appear on your official transcript of credits. They'll be but signs of heart and mind: respect for intellectual inquiry, precision of thought and expression, prudent judgment. This is a goodly heritage. I know you'll guard it jealously.

As my previous remarks indicate, I believe Huron College discharges its obligations to students with high distinction. On an annual operating budget no larger than would be spent in producing a grade-B horror movie, the institution serves the youth of this plains region, as well as more distant areas. In 1956, one of America's large corporations spent more than fifteen times as much on advertising as has been spent in the operation of this college throughout its entire history. I submit that the 1,300 or so graduates, not to mention the several thousands who didn't complete their degrees, demonstrate that Huron College has been able to turn out quality products on so-called low-cost budgets.

Through dedicated service of administrators and teachers, students have been guided fruitfully in matters of the intellect and the spirit. Huron College has immeasurably enriched the lives of competent, deserving young men and women by opening doors of learning, and providing friendly passage for all who were of serious intent. Moreover, the influence of this college has always touched parents as well as students. During my time at the college—and this is doubtless still true—many of us came from homes in which the parents had not had extensive schooling. But they had an abiding faith, even though not well-defined, in the value of higher education. The friendliness of Huron's teachers and administrators toward them, the apparent worth of what their sons and daughters were being taught, and the character of the final product at the end of the four-year stay generally justified their faith, a faith that often had to survive the severest possible test of economic sacrifice. These parents became firm supporters of the enterprise of learning, even though they took no direct part in it. I would urge that no one underestimate this influence of a college. Even today there are persons who hold intellectual achievement in contempt.

Now a final word to the graduating class.

Some years ago, a Texas cowboy took a job in Arizona. His first order from the new boss was to ride out on the range and find some cattle that had strayed from the herd. Suddenly and quite unexpectedly, he found himself on the south rim of the Grand Canyon. No one had told him there was a canyon, and he had never heard of it. Wide-eyed and almost horror-stricken, he looked into this fantastic abyss, wiped his forehead, and said: "Good heavens! Something has happened here."

Something has also happened *here* during your stay at the college. Profound changes have taken place in you: in your beliefs, your attitudes, your point of view, your ways of meeting problems in private and public life.

I remember the sound advice that President George Shannon McCune gave me when I was a freshman. His words were symbolic of the service this college offers its students. Thinking perhaps that I was among the greenest and most ill-adjusted of the freshmen—a conclusion I'm not prepared to refute—Dr. McCune called me to his office shortly before the Thanksgiving recess. Briefly, here's what he said: "Soon you'll be going home for the first time since you came to college. Even though you've been here less than three months, Huron has had an influence on you. When you get home, you'll find that some of the things your folks think important won't seem so to you; and some things you take pretty seriously, will seem foolish to them. Just remember: They haven't changed since you left, but you have."

I can offer no wiser counsel. You probably won't fully appreciate the magnitude of the changes until you've been away from the college for several years. But to deny that they've taken place will be as futile as to argue with the west wind.

With this day, my friends, you enter upon the more complete management of your own affairs. I know you'll meet your enlarged responsibilities with good spirit, humility, and loyalty to high ideals and standards, knowing, with Joseph Addison, that "a man's first care should be to avoid the reproaches of his own heart." I congratulate you upon your graduation, and I wish you well.

EDUCATION FOR MULTIPLE LEADERSHIP [9]

ROBERT J. BLAKELY [10]

Robert J. Blakely, vice president of the Fund for Adult Education of the Ford Foundation, gave this address to the Conference on Continuing Education, at Kellogg Center, Michigan State University, East Lansing, June 15, 1958.

Blakely joined the staff of the newly created Fund for Adult Education in 1951, as manager of the Central Regional Office. He became vice president in 1956.

Prominent in Blakely's activities for the Fund has been his public speaking; in constant demand as a speaker, he has appeared in almost every state and in Canada. He has also talked frequently over radio and television. He has established himself as one of the nation's leading speakers on education, and he is the outstanding speaker on adult education.

Although each speech is strikingly original, his themes are basically the same—the worth of the individual, the threats to and the dangers of freedom, the responsibility of each citizen, and the need for democratic leadership. His thought is incisive and provocative, his proofs logical, motivative, and strongly persuasive; his language firm, fresh, sometimes poetic; his speech structure orderly, relevant, and climactic. His style is that of enlightened journalism. (He was formerly editorial writer on the Des Moines *Register* and the St. Louis *Star Times.*) His delivery is precise and intellectual, but communicative and extempore even when a manuscript is before him. This speaker's personality explains much of his effectiveness—his mental acuteness and integrity, conscience, directness of purpose and method, moral vitality.[11]

A volume of Blakely's recent speeches has been published under the title *Adult Education in a Free Society* by J. R. Kidd, Canadian manager of the Fund.

The trouble with most discussions of education is that they do not deal with things which are essential, which we care about deeply, which excite the mind, quicken the heart and twinge the bowels. Matters of curriculum, method, teachers, buildings, finance—these and other such are important, but they are *deriva-*

[9] Text with permission for this reprint furnished by Robert J. Blakely.

[10] For biographical note, see Appendix.

[11] For further comment on Blakely as a speaker, see the Cumulative Author Index for references to his speeches in earlier volumes.

tive. They derive from the *purpose* of education; this in turn derives from, or better, perhaps, is a part of the nature of the culture or civilization which education serves. (By "culture" I mean the relatively simple, so-called "primitive" societies, by "civilization" the relatively complex, so-called "advanced" societies.)

Man has a very small capacity for instinct and a very large capacity to learn. He has been given to know few things through that mysterious transmission labeled "instinct." He has to learn almost everything. And, emancipated by his helplessness, he can learn almost everything. Genetically, man is more similar than any other species; behaviorally, man is more various than any other species.

A culture or civilization is a way of life. This way of life gives coherence to the different aspects of living and direction to development. It shapes the members and the generations. At the root of a culture or civilization is an outlook, guided by a set of values.

Education in any culture or civilization is the purposeful activity by which the members inculcate the basic values and focus the orienting outlook. Of course, while and after this is done, supporting attitudes need to be fashioned and enabling skills need to be taught, but the guiding values and the basic outlook are at the root of the culture or civilization, and they are at the heart of education within a culture or civilization. This basic outlook and set of values usually get neglected in consideration of education.

Simple or "primitive" cultures have no formal institutions known as schools. Education is conducted in all ways and always. It is conducted in the home, in tribal rituals, in work, in play, in warfare. It operates upon the members of the society from the day they are born until the day they are buried, and the very ceremonies of birth and death are themselves educational exercises.

The Soviet system aspires to be, not just a state, a government, but a way of life—a civilization. Therefore, *consciously* using all devices which a simple culture uses unconsciously, it seeks to set the basic values and to orient the outlook of its members in all ways and always: in the home, through work and play, in military service, by means of the mass media, above all through the political party, which is both a skeleton and a neural scheme: not just through the schools; not just during the years when young people are in school. This I will amplify later.

What of the United States? Is it a way of life, a civilization? I answer, yes. If I am right, and if my thesis about civilizations is correct, then there must be an orienting outlook directed by a basic set of values. What gives it coherence at any one time? What gives it direction in history? I suggest that it is what we at least point to when we use such shorthand phrases as "the worth of the individual," "the dignity of the individual," "the individual as an end in his own right," "the infinite potentiality of the individual"—these and other inadequate phrases. This, if anything, is our basic value, and our orienting outlook is set according to it. To say so much is not to say that we do not have other values and other views. But if there is one ideal which has given coherence in space and time to the American civilization, it is this. At the crucial moments—the revolt against colonialism, the creation of the federation, the survival of federation against secession, the taming of corporate power, the assimilation of immigrants, the invention of "people's capitalism" —this ideal and only this ideal has given commonality and direction. It gives us whatever coherence and whatever sense of direction we have today.

The outlook is an open, or, better, an *opening* outlook, regarding knowledge as tentative and expanding, the actual as merely indicative of the potential, the individual and the society as infinitely improvable.

Now this regard for the individual does not mean that all impulses of the individual are of equal value. It does not mean that all corridors for the development of potentialities are equally promising. It does not mean that if society tries through education to cultivate certain impulses and to curb others that it is denying the openness and the worth of the individual. If we agree that the basic value of our civilization is respect for the individual, then we have to ask: "What are the conditions under which the individual, each individual, *all* individuals have the greatest opportunity to develop their capacities?" We have to ask further, "What are the qualities and capacities of human beings which make this possible and which we want to encourage? And what are the qualities and capacities we want to discourage through our education?" And after we've answered this, we have to ask: "How can we produce the desired kind or kinds of persons? How can we produce them in all ways, not just through our schools, but by means of all of the influences that play upon people? And how can we do it, not just in the period of life from the fifth year through the twenty-second or twenty-third or twenty-fourth year or whenever formal schooling ends, but throughout the whole range of life, from birth until death—just as does the primitive society and just as the Soviet civilization is trying to do?"

Many of the difficulties of the present condition of American life flow, it seems to me, from three related facts. First, we have lost sight of our basic values. Second, we have assigned education to a single institution, the schools, thereby giving the schools an impossible task and stripping other institutions of educative roles. A consequence of this is, of course, that we have assigned education to a few hours of the days of a few years and made the other hours of the days of the years of our lives uneducative. Third, we have become preoccupied with secondary purposes unrelated to primary purposes. Most of our education is concerned with knowledge or skills for *particular functions* of the individual or with the needs of *particular institutions* and is not addressed to the basic concern of how to produce the kinds of people we need to produce the kind of society we want.

I illustrate by reference to the American people's reaction to the achievements of the Soviet Union in rocketry. We felt that something had gone wrong, that we were falling behind. The first utterances were a spate of alarms calling for more mathematicians, scientists and technicians. Then came many heartening replies, saying that more than an arms race is at stake—that a conception of man and the good life is at stake; but what is needed is not just more scientists and technicians but more well-educated people in all areas of life. Many of these statements were good statements. But not a major statement did I see which held up the conception of education as the responsibility, not just of the schools, but of all the aspects of society, and a job not just for the school years, but for the whole sweep of life's span.

For a time our schools were made a whipping boy. And then what happened? Well, inasfar as anything has happened, I fear it has been what the first alarmists called for—a heavier and narrower stress upon science, mathematics and technology, without even a broad and profound understanding of the cultural and intellectual foundations of these.

This raises the question of leadership. For the rest of this speech I am going to talk about education for leadership in a free society.

Many Americans—particularly leaders—feel uneasy talking about leadership. The smell of *Der Führer* and *Il Duce* is still upon the word. I would like to avoid, if possible, the charge that I am advocating a philosophy of the elite. I assert again that in our society the individual is the end—each individual, all individuals; and the goal is equal opportunities for all to develop themselves to their highest reach. I assert again that what matters in the long run is not achievements in the sciences or even in the arts, nor is it physical standards of living (that is, beyond that margin above subsistence that makes it possible for us to be human); what matters is the quality of the lives of people. And self-government is the best kind of government because it is a means for the exercise of the capacities of individuals as ends. But after this is said, I, at least, find it necessary to return to the ideas of leadership and authority.

Authority is another word which has fallen on evil days. Much thinking in the United States—particularly in the field of adult education—has confused authority with authoritarianism. Authority is always necessary. It should not always be exercised, but it should always be possible. The one sure way for a person or a society always to be wrong is not to be able to decide or to execute a decision. Often it is not wise to force an issue, but the decision not to do so should be in itself a decision. The best kind of authority is what we mean when, as in scholarship, we say, "He speaks with authority," meaning, "He knows what he is talking about." Even under tyranny authority ultimately rests, if not upon consent, at least upon acceptance. In a free society the necessary degree of voluntary acceptance and willing consent is high. The questions are, is authority in the good sense offered? And, if offered, is it respected and recognized?

Leadership and followership imply each other. In a free society there are many kinds of leadership; there are many roles of leadership; there are many places in which leadership is given. In a free society there are many kinds of followership, many roles of followership, and many places in which followership is given. In a free society there are much change and interplay in the roles of followership and leadership.

When this process works well, at a particular time and in a particular situation the appropriate kind of leadership is offered, recognized and followed—this changing imperceptibly as the time and the situation change. To my mind comes the memory of a display of aurora borealis. Streamers from all points in the horizon met in the infinite; the focus of the infinite harrowed the heavens; the spectrum of colors distinguished, combined, dissolved, and distinguished again. There was a thrilling presence of illimitable energy, colors far beyond the slitted human capacity to see, sounds too vast for dullness of the human ear.

This should be contrasted to the rigidities of a totalitarian system like the Soviet system. As I shall later say, I take its challenge very seriously. But ultimately it has a fatal defect. Leadership concentrates, in a few from the beginning, then inescapably in Number One. First the few, then the One must be expert in all things—science, art, economics, politics, war. Denying the many their birthright to be human, first the few and finally Number One must play God. Human attempts to be God always result in subhumanity.

For a free society to survive and prevail over a totalitarian society its people need to be, not superhuman but high-order human. They need to use excellence of many kinds from many people in many situations.

What is the American attitude toward excellence? It is certainly ambivalent. We prize excellence in surgery when our child is being operated upon. We prize excellence on the concert stage or on the baseball diamond, if we enjoy music and sports.

But we tend to resent excellence in others when they are competing with us for things we want. This was noted a long time ago, perhaps first by de Tocqueville, who studied the United States shortly after the Jacksonian revolution. He noted that many forces in democracy in America pressed toward uniformity and mediocrity.

This is not inherent in the theory of democracy. Jefferson, for example, recognzed and sought to encourage "the natural aristocracy of virtue and talent." He saw the essence of democracy, not in the denial of excellence, but in the opportunity for the development and use of excellence *wherever it may be,* regardless of origin or circumstance.

A regard for excellence is not opposed to a regard for individuality. Quite the contrary. In mediocrity we are like most others. In excellence we are always individual. In deferring to excellence in others we are not surrendering our individuality. We are, instead, sharing by entering into a relationship with it.

In my judgment the forces pressing toward uniformity and mediocrity and against excellence are increasing in the United States. This is deleterious to the quality of our personal lives. It is deleterious also to the making and execution of the policies of the American people, internal and external, at home and abroad. Here we mount a plain which is more than a matter of taste—more than a preference for the comfort of dealing with people "just like ourselves" to the discomfort of being in the presence of that which exceeds us. At stake on this plain is the survival and future of the United States, the survival and future of the idea of freedom as the good life, perhaps, even the survival and freedom of the human race.

In this context, let us compare how the Soviet system and the American system educate for leadership.

I deal first with the Soviet system. I do not need to specify the Soviets' accomplishments in science and technology; the massive rockets in their complex orbits are visible symbols. I do not need to specify their accomplishments in industry, with productivity increasing at the rate of 7 per cent compared to our 4 per cent, and with little of this going into chromium on automobiles or deep freezes in which to keep forgotten foods. I do not need to specify to you their achievements in mobilizing the energies of the Soviet people; we are, I think, very much out of date if we continue to regard the Soviet people just as cattle being driven unwillingly down the road. The Soviet system to a remarkable degree has managed to win the dedication of its people, harnessing something very important to human beings—the desire to affiliate with larger than personal purposes. And I do not need to develop at any length the achievements of the Soviet system abroad. Somehow or other, despite what it did to Czechoslovakia in 1948, despite what it did to the Hungarian people in 1956, nevertheless the Soviet Union has been able to identify itself in the minds of hundreds of millions of people in the world wth the goals of peace, justice, economic aid and technical assistance. And when the Soviets send technicians to India, for example, they send people who not only can perform technically but also can speak the colloquial languages and live at ease with them in their mud huts or under their thatched roofs.

The accomplishments of the Soviets seriously raise a question which for generations we in the United States thought had received a final answer—that is whether the freedom of the individual is the best basis for releasing human talents and organizing human energies. We can no longer take it for granted that the answer is yes. If the answer *is* yes, this must be proved by successful demonstration.

Behind the sharp nose-cone of Soviet abilities is the thrust of purpose. The purpose is guided by an outlook which views the triumph of the Communist cause as inevitable. The thrust is powered by basic values which idolize the state and immolate individuals to service and sacrifice. Service and sacrifice are employed by a single organization—the party. And all this is efficiently furthered by the Soviet educational system.

We in the West have had opportunity in recent months to learn much about the Soviet educational system—through several books and through the reports of numerous visits. For the purposes of the Communist leaders it is a good educational system. There is universal compulsory education of young people through the seventh year. Then elaborate tests are given. On the bases of these tests, some youngsters "volunteer" for agricultural work, others "volunteer" for industrial work, and so on. Those who are the ablest (and who are not politically suspect) are chosen for the areas of science and technology, the military, education and government. (Government, of course, is all the functions of the party-state.) The advanced education given these chosen ones is apparently good education—solid, wide-ranging and integrated. You are out of date if you think that the educated Communist is a parrot with blinders. The educated Communist is deeply rooted in Communist values and firmly oriented according to Communist views. But, this granted, he is widely informed and intellectually adroit, particularly in dialectical discussion and propagandistic debate. The Soviet system has deliberate, systematic preparation for the leadership it must depend upon.

I am going to raise two questions, just for recognition, not for development. The first: Is there not a fatal weakness in a system in which power concentrates ultimately in one office, for which the only schooling is the curriculum of the jungle? The second: Is it possible for a system based on a single deterministic philosophy to maintain itself as it gives basic education to all its people and advanced education first to tens of thousands and soon to millions of its ablest people? These questions, I think, point to the two Achilles' heels of the Soviet system. But we cannot placidly count upon these vulnerabilities. With regard to the first question, we should remember that Adolf Hitler, knowing he was doomed, chose to take as many people with him as possible. Suppose he had had intercontinental fusion-bomb rockets. With regard to the second possibility, either the Soviet system would gradually become more liberal, in which case the West should be ready with encouragement, or it would go to pieces, certainly explosively, in which case the West should be ready with affirmative alternatives, not for its own advantage, but primarily for the benefit of the Soviet peoples.

Both the "shoulds" in the "either" and the "or" of the last sentence ask a good bit of man who is born of woman and who has a common ancestry with the shrew. But are there any other promising forks in the road ahead? And, what does "civilization" mean except to make great demands upon the descendant of the shrew?

With this in mind, I turn now to the American system.

In contrast to the Soviets' sole philosophy, the American people have many philosophies. Some say we have—and *must have*—no philosophy. These exult in multiplicity, in differences, in pluralism. So do I. But to have pluralism and *no* philosophy is impossible. Pluralism requires a philosophy. In the outer regions of space, where hydrogen atoms tiredly collide, no environment is necessary. But on the planet Earth, which, despite the statistics of probability, may still be the curvedly infinite universe's only host to what we call life, pluralism requires an ecology. Ecology means a workable "co-existence" of living things in their environment. To leap to the point, what are the circumstances within which it is possible for human beings "to agree to disagree agreeably"? These are much more subtle, delicate and complex than the circumstances which relate women (who keep cats, which kill rats, which eat the eggs of bumblebees, which fertilize red clover) and red clover. We must work, and work hard, to establish and maintain the commonalities which make pluralism possible.

In contrast to the Soviet system's single organization, we in the United States have many organizations. Government at different levels; separation of powers; two major parties; the threat or promise of minor parties; organizations according to economic interests; organizations according to intellectual interests; affiliations of associations; associations of asociations; the society for the advancement of extrasensory perception; the committee for the preservation of the addle-pated egret. These are merely flavors of the richness of what it means to be free to associate. The heart of the matter can be described in two ways. First, decision-making is decentralized, dispersed, diffused, shared. Second, the state, instead of being the origin or the permitter of other organizations, is the *consequence* of voluntary associations. This is the ideal. The quality of the reality and the survival of the reality depends on how morally and wisely this dispersed authority is used. This means leadership.

In the American society leadership is multiple: Different kinds—intellectual, moral, financial, political, "charismatic." Leadership is needed from the solitary creator. It is needed in many organizations of many kinds. Within these many organizations it is needed at various levels. In the American society leaders often, indeed, usually, play several roles. Sometimes these are sequential, with a person moving from post to post. Sometimes these are simultaneous, with a person carrying several responsibilities. Many, perhaps, despite the growth of formal government, most of our affairs are still conducted through informal organizations. Positions of policy-making are frequently filled, not with experts, but with lay persons.

One day in Des Moines a mysterious visit was paid to my editor, W. W. Waymack, by David Lilienthal. A week later Waymack was a member of the Atomic Energy Commission. This illustrates the unpredictable responsibilities which fall to the lot of the citizens of a free society.

And—to come to the point—in the United States we have no systematic organized program of continuing education of our mature citizens for public responsibilities.

For smaller responsibilities we have many programs—for management, for shop stewards, for county agents; for accounting, for law, for first aid. You name it. We got it. But there are sharp teeth in the old saw, "Everybody's cat is nobody's cat"; we have no systematic attention to education for large overriding all-encompassing public responsibilities.

Let me not overstate the case. In business there is a growing number of educational programs aimed at liberal or general education. In labor increasing attention is being given to the education of members of unions as individuals and as citizens. In the Cooperative Agricultural Extension Service efforts are being made to broaden the educational opportunities for rural people. A ferment is at work in public schools, universities and colleges, libraries, museums, and voluntary organizations responding to the recognition that special abilities, private concerns and secondary purposes are not enough. All this and other evidences of vitality in our society which could be marshaled are encouraging. If the American people could expect a century like the one which England enjoyed after the Napoleonic wars, we could be justifiably confident. But no such century can be reasonably foreseen.

Therefore, the call is loud and clear to the American people for a vigorous and imaginative system of continuing education for its adults, preparing them to meet the responsibilities which are theirs.

Such program should pay special attention to those persons who are already in positions of grave responsibility and to those who are likely to occupy such positions in the next five to fifteen years. But just as, in the words of Old Walt, "Great artists need great audiences," so do educated leaders need educated followers. And in our society, who can tell who will be called upon to lead?

To make this point vivid, I relate a story. When "Skip" Graham, of the Louisville, Kentucky, Public Library, was president of the American Library Association, he called upon President Harry Truman to urge support of a bill to aid libraries. In his breezy way he began the conversation by saying, "Mr. Truman, as one president to another . . ." As soon as Mr. Truman learned the point of the conversation, he said, "You need say no more. Except for law, most of what I have learned I learned through the public library." Ever since hearing this story I have looked with a fresh and respectful eye upon the men and women reading in the public libraries I visit.

A system of educational programs should stress those whose decisions do or may have wide consequences. But it cannot be limited to these. Nothing will be adequate except that which is as broad as our extension of self-government and as continuous as the demands that are being made upon us for courage and wisdom.

Henry David Thoreau wrote:

> We spend more on almost any article of bodily aliment or ailment than on our mental aliment. It is time that we had uncommon schools, that we did not leave off our education when we begin to be men and women. It is time that villages were universities, and their elder inhabitants the fellows of universities, with leisure—if they are, indeed, so well

off—to pursue liberal studies the rest of their lives. . . . If we live in the nineteenth century, why should we not enjoy the advantages which the nineteenth century offers? Why should our life be in any respect provincial?

If more than a century ago it was time "that we did not leave off our education when we begin to be men and women," it is far past time today. If the advantages of the nineteenth century made it unnecessary for free men and women to be provincial, the advantages and the requirements of the second half of the twentieth century make it criminal to be provincial.

A civilization has been defined as a shared ideal. Ortega y Gasset in *Invertebrate Spain* wrote that a people do not come together and stay together just in order to be together; they do so only if they have a project in common.

The project that the American people have in common is the building of a society in which the worth of the individual is valued. We now intimately share the earth and, also the heavens, with all other peoples of the planet. What is the project in common which will make it possible for mankind to come together and stay together in peace and creativity? It can be no other than the same ideal of the value of the individual.

These were my thoughts yesterday, Flag Day, when, driving from Willow Run, I heard over the car radio that thrilling poem "The New Colossus" by Emma Lazarus, to be read within the Statue of Liberty:

> . . . "Give me your tired, your poor,
> Your huddled masses yearning to breathe free,
> The wretched refuse of your teeming shore.
> Send these, the homeless, tempest-tost to me,
> I lift my lamp beside the golden door!"

What a mockery of this our immigration policies are. How apt it is that, instead of Ellis Island's being made into a shrine, it is likely to be made into a warehouse or a mental hospital.

We cannot, of course, take all peoples into our continent, but we can take them all into our minds and our hearts. Enlargement of the mind and heart is one way of stating the objectives of education for freedom. And, just as the responsibilities of freedom continually grow, so must we continually enlarge ourselves through education.

Basically, perhaps, the reason the Russian people are so interested in education is that they are eager to bring the future into being. Basically, perhaps, the reason the American people neglect education is that we are afraid of the future. We must once again become confident that we can influence the future. The values at the heart of American civilization—regard for the worth of each human being—give us a project we can hold in common with the entire human race.

RELIGION

A CALL TO SELF-DISCIPLINE [1]

JOSEPH RICHARD SIZOO [2]

The Reverend Dr. Joseph R. Sizoo, Milbank Professor of Religion at George Washington University, Washington, D.C., gave this sermon to the graduating class on June 1, 1958.

Dr. Sizoo is one of the nation's foremost preachers, and was for ten years pastor of New York City's St. Nicholas Collegiate Church; a scholar and teacher, and president of the New Brunswick Theological seminary for five years, he is the author of numerous works on religious themes.

The address followed Sizoo's typical methods of sermonizing. The organization and development of his ideas were clear cut. The vivid analysis of the problem of an undisciplined age was followed by explanations of the avenues through which self-discipline is to be strengthened: political, intellectual, and moral. Sizoo gave chief emphasis to this hard view of self-discipline. He enforced his propositions with many concrete references or quotations, citing the Declaration of Independence, Little Rock, the "Edith" of a recent novel, Shakespeare, Karl Marx, the Bible, college teachers, *Dear Brutus,* a Vachel Lindsey poem, and Richard Watson Gilder. The address was contemporary in its allusions, attention-holding for college students. It was composed and delivered with much inspirational purpose and method.

Mr. President, members of the graduating class:

A person's value to society is determined not by the things he begins but by the things he ends, not by the forces he sets in motion but by the forces he brings to a successful conclusion. Anybody can begin a thing but to bring it to a successful end reveals the earmarks of a worth-while life in the eyes of God and history. What a satisfaction therefore these days must bring to you. What you have begun you have ended, and the forces you have set in motion you have brought to a successful conclusion. I join your friends in extending you greetings and congratulations.

[1] Text furnished by Dr. Joseph R. Sizoo, with permission for this reprint.
[2] For biographical note, see Appendix.

We live today in a period of history marked by distinctive and disturbing characteristics. No one can call himself a discerning student of contemporary life unless he lives with an awareness of them. We speak of this as the unpredictable age: anything can happen, nothing is impossible, nothing stays put. We refer to it as the atomic age. Words like satellite, intercontinental missile, electric charges, space ships, and atomic fission are breathing down our necks. Forces never before known have become commonplace; techniques and disciplines never available to any man have suddenly become available to all men. Some refer to this as the age of the ulcer: a devasting neurosis is biting into the life of modern man. But perhaps the most sobering characteristic of our time and surely its greatest peril is the lost sense of discipline. A blatant unrestraint has taken hold of people.

This is an era when people are swerving from high purpose, accommodating themselves to what is expedient and convenient. They follow the line of least resistance. They never take sides, they never put a trumpet to their lips, they never unfurl a flag, they never commit themselves to anything, they never respond to a call. They have a way of pigeonholing an inconvenient conscience. They gyrate from one side of the street to the other, depending upon where the sun is shining. They send up a trial balloon to find out which way the wind is blowing before they give an expression to an opinion. They are afraid of the black mark of public disapproval. They let *I will* wait upon *I would.* They are terrorized by a shower of postcards and a wheelbarrow of telegrams.

This is the most devasting threat to modern society. Thoreau once wrote, "Youth gets together his materials to build a bridge to the moon, or perchance, a palace or temple on the earth, and at length the middle-aged man concludes to build a woodshed with them." That middle-aged mind and spread has taken hold of many today. They want what they want as they want it and when they want it. They throw all discretion to the wind and are utterly unconcerned about the consequences of their deeds upon others. Step by step, gradually and perhaps unwittingly, they accept and acquiesce in elements which involve compromise.

All around us one sees cynical indifference, tolerance of lies, and decay of honesty coupled with whining self-pity.

If imagination, daring, and courage are necessary for the building of a new world, surely these cannot be developed in men who are soft, indulgent, flabby, and pampered by circumstances. We shall never build a better tomorrow until we have a baptism of self-discipline.

Let me point to some areas in modern life in which all this is relevant.

1. You must help your age recover the sense of self-discipline on the national level. The desire for freedom goes deep with us. We take rather seriously the Declaration of Independence "that all men are created free and equal." We have a passion for freedom in this country. But the blunt fact is that freedom is having a hard time to survive. It seems like a lonely island in a sea of hate and suspicion. We are no longer first in scientific genius, and no longer first in the hearts of men. The high regard which people of the world have always had for us is rapidly fading into the mists of suspicion and misgivings. How can you account for that and what explains it? Can it be that the principles which have always undergirded and sustained freedom: service, responsibility, mutual respect, religious tolerance, racial good will, and economic justice, have been brushed aside and pushed against the wall while we have substituted for them other principles: demanding rights, self-interest, pressure groups, political double talk, Little Rock, indifference to education? And can it be that when once again we have disciplined our freedom restoring economic, social, religious, and racial tolerance and good will that freedom's holy light will once again shine across the earth?

Freedom is like a coin. It has the word privilege on one side and responsibility on the other. It does not have privilege on both sides. There are too many today who want everything involved in privilege but refuse to accept anything that approaches the sense of responsibility. A modern novelist in one of the recent books has a character called Edith. The novelist describes Edith in this fashion: "Edith is a little country bounded on the north and on the south, on the east and on the west by Edith."

The signs multiply that we are becoming crass and banal and undisciplined, coupled with an epidemic of unreason. Walls always buckle when foundations crumble. It is still true that eternal vigilance is the price of freedom. If freedom is to survive in the world of tomorrow, we shall need to cleanse and purify it. Perhaps that is your first assignment with destiny.

2. You must help your age recover the sense of self-discipline on the intellectual level. In the area of learning there is so much contentment today with mediocrity and the superficial. Our generation has no desire to go deep in knowledge. Scholarship, which requires hard study and long hours, is frowned upon by those who want to stand well with the group. Bookishness is twisted to mean freakishness and to make a fast buck is more important than learning history.

You stand at opposite poles from all that. Your university has fixed standards which never compromise with mediocrity. Your very presence here bears witness to your intellectual competence. You may go out in the world unashamed and unafraid. But there is so little of that in modern life.

Because many refuse to live with the discipline of the mind they have developed all manner of short cuts to learning. We have dehydrated Shakespeare; we have Karl Marx for children; we have history in pictures; we have the Bible in comic strips. Learn a foreign language in six lessons or your money back! It is the age of the short poem, the one-act play, and digest form of novels. Our thinking has bogged down since Fulton, Edison, Brashear, and Steinmetz led the nation to inventive genius. It is said that more than one fourth of the high schools in the United States do not have courses in science. When you try to find out why that is the answer is always, "It is too hard."

We have developed a hit and run concept of education. The school has become a sort of intellectual hot dog stand where no one tarries very long, except to get a quick bite, gulped down with breeze courses and academic hoopla as they rush off to the next attraction. This is the age of butterfly learning; we flutter everywhere, sipping a little here and sipping a little there, but settling nowhere. We string poles and wires from coast to coast; we have vastly improved the techniques and mechanics of communication, but we have so little to communicate. Believe me, there is no short cut to learning for everything has its price. If we are to give leadership and direction to the world of tomorrow, we must restore the discipline of learning. This too is your assignment with destiny.

3. There is a third area in which all this is relevant. You must restore self-discipline in the moral order. This whole business of evading unpleasant assignments, sidestepping reponsibilities, and dodging issues bears witness to the blatant unrestraint of modern man. There is so much accommodation to what is comfortable, convenient, and expedient. When issues arise, they hold aloof and like the Pharisees of old pass by on the other side. When some cause solicits their interest, they wrap themselves up in dry ice. When some crusade is launched, they let the armies march by. On the stage of the world they refuse to be actors; they are content to sit in the balcony eating peanuts, shrugging their shoulders with, "What is the use; if I don't do it somebody else will; we are a long time dead, and a hundred years from now nobody will know the difference."

I asked a group not long ago involved in a dreadful delinquency, "Why did you do this?" Their answer was, "Frankly we do not care for things like that; we have no heart for them." I asked them, "Why then did you do it?" They answered, "We do not want to stand out like a sore thumb." When the philosophy, "They all do it," takes root and man resigns his moral control to the crowd, the inevitable next step is anarchy.

Here is a teacher who frankly permits cheating to go unchallenged. He suggests that if he taught honesty it would not prepare the student for life. Indeed, "to teach honesty would give him a false orientation. Honesty is not realistic." Here is a popular tragic personality involved in a tragic death, under even more tragic circumstances, assured that all this is no cause for either regret or embarrassment; it will increase the box office returns.

The want of moral fiber is leaving its marks on life today. The signs multiply of a soggy moral standard. It is popular to disclaim all moral responsibility for everything. We blame criminal behavior on heredity, neighborhood conditions, family maladjustments, sex, libido, or some other hocus-pocus; everywhere, except where it belongs, personal moral responsibility. James Barrie in his *Dear Brutus* portrays a group of unhappy disillusioned people in an English home. If only the setting of their lives had been different, if only they had had other talents and other work to do, then indeed they would have known serenity and happiness. The butler was sure he would be happy if he had been a financier; the sculptor is positive he would have had great joy in life if only he had been a painter. So the hostess arranges for them to change to the status in which they believed they would find happiness. The sculptor becomes a painter, and the butler becomes a financier, and so on. The fact, however, is that the sculptor on becoming a painter lost all sense of genius and inspiration. The butler had become rich, but his great riches had made him coarse and crude. In the end they all revert to the same status of unhappiness and disillusionment with which they had come to the English home. So James Barrie, with an innate genius, concludes the play with, "The fault, dear Brutus, is not in our stars, but in ourselves."

It is significant that an era which refuses to accept the disciplines of life is in such desperate search for serenity and strength. An age which seeks to find serenity by tranquilizing pills, sleeping on foam mattresses, counting sheep, and buying peace of mind books written by this or that swami with or without turbans, has yet to learn that the sooner we stop fooling with the Ten Commandments and the arithmetic table will we experience those inner resources of peace which come alone through obedience to the will and the law of God. The greatest single need of our time is to reassert and reaffirm those basic realities which have disciplined men in the past. A distinguished American has indeed spoken wisely, "We have grasped the mystery of the atom, but we have rejected the Sermon on the Mount. We have achieved brillance without wisdom, and power without conscience. Ours is a world of nuclear giants and ethical infants." We have become spiritual albinos whose mortal clay has been bleached but in which there has not yet been breathed the breath of life. We need people in education, in legislation, in busness who believe in a moral order that is centered in God.

The moment a civilization loses touch with God life becomes so complex and complicated men do not know how to handle it or what to make of it.

If ever we fall apart and lose our freedom and leadership, it will not be because we lack political technique, social patterns, and economic regulations, but because we refused to discipline ourselves. When the roots wither, the tree perishes. You cannot build a new world by stringing together a great number of bad people.

If the need of our time does not turn on programs but on people with self-respect enough to be servants of eternal purpose rather than straws in the wind of circumstance, if our difficulties are not so much political and economic as moral and spiritual, then only by a fresh awareness of God can we stop this modern social and political decay and place life on the basis of soundness and decency.

We have changed from sailing ships to jet airliners, from hieroglyphics to electric typewriters, from clay tablets to Oxford editions, from mud huts to penthouses, but to what end? What is the good of a civilization whose art ends in comic strips, whose music ends in rock 'n' roll, whose learning ends in red-back-magazine stories of smutted lives and soiled tempers coated over with psychoanalysis and tossed off as literature, whose science ends in the capacity of self-destruction? Education may rationalize life, government may nationalize life, business may mechanize life, but only religion can spiritualize life. Vachel Lindsey wrote it for us in these words,

> Not that they starve, but starve so drearily,
> Not that they sow, but that they never reap,
> Not that they serve, but have no Gods to serve,
> Not that they die, but that they die like sheep.

Across the lonely centuries there comes once again the voice of the Son of Man, "Seek ye first the kingdom of God and its righteousness and all these things shall be added unto you."

This is your world; it is the only world you will ever know. If you ever expect to do anything for it, it will have to be in that kind of a setting. You did not make that world, but you have the chance to do something about it. Whether this fills you with fear or with adventure, whether that makes your blood run cold or your nerves tingle, depends entirely on the stuff of which you are made.

In a few days you will leave this intellectual home in which you have lived these happy years. It is quite possible that you will feel like the little bear who ran away from his mother determined to live his own life at his own convenience. When he got to the top of a nearby hill and saw peak after peak and valley after valley stretch on and on and on to the far off horizons, he rushed back to his mother and said, "The world is so large; take me back, I am afraid."

Surely you will not run back. As a matter of fact, they won't take you back. You are starting the journey, and you will go on and on. It is an entrancing and difficult journey. It is entrancing because it will bring you glorious opportunities, high romance, great adventure, independence, and joy unspeakable. It will also be difficult because the grandeur will often be corroded by cruelty and stupidity and evil. The world will try to take away your happiness, rob you of your integrity, break your heart, and hang a cross on your back. Richard Watson Gilder in his "Ode to Grover Cleveland" wrote a solemn warning, "Lonely is the life that listens to no voice save that of duty." You can either stand up to that world and pay the price or you can yield to that world and let it bend you. If you do the latter, you will never again be able to look yourself or your university in the face. But that is your choice. Some of you will fail, some of you will triumph, but all of you must struggle in this battle where character is made.

The eyes of those who hope for a better world are turned to people like you. God forbid you should trail in the dust their golden hopes.

Members of the graduating class of 1958 I salute you.

THE GREATNESS OF LINCOLN [3]

RICHARD S. EMRICH [4]

The Reverend Richard S. Emrich, Episcopal Bishop of Michigan, gave this sermon in the Washington Cathedral, Washington, D.C., on January 11, 1959, in observance of the Lincoln sesquicentennial celebration. The occasion was a special service in which the bishop of Washington, D.C., also participated. It was attended by Vice President Richard M. Nixon, members of the Lincoln Sesquicentennial Commission, and a large congregation. United Nations Under-Secretary Ralph J. Bunche and Senator John Sherman Cooper of Kentucky read the Scripture lessons for the service.

The sermon was one of the outstanding and more permanent addresses on the subject. Bishop Emrich, presenting a philosophical analysis and interpretation of Lincoln, achieved originality of expression and thought as he reviewed three aspects of Lincoln's greatness: (1) his "Olympian outlook" on mankind; (2) his method of reasoning; and (3) his religious stature. The perspicuity and dignity of the Bishop's rhetorical invention, his sermonic structure and style, and his measured and flexible delivery combined to produce a sermon that was, as Senator Cooper described it, "learned, eloquent, and moving."

My friends, I count it one of the privileges of my life to speak to you on this occasion. I do not know any more about Abraham Lincoln than most of you here, and I know far less than some of you; but I will affirm that I love the man, and that wisdom and the grace of God have come to me through him.

Our text is the well-known statement of our Lord, "By their fruits shall ye know them."

It is common knowledge that when one stands too close to a mountain range, one cannot see which mountain is the highest and towers above the rest. It is only at a distance that a true perspective is gained, and the great peak can be distinguished from the foothills. So it was that some who lived close to Lincoln could not see his greatness, and failed to see which speech was great at Gettysburg. So it is that we, 150 years after his birth,

[3] Text furnished by Bishop Richard E. Emrich, with permission for this reprint. Reprinted also in the *Congressional Record*. 105:A694-5 (daily edition). February 2, 1959.

[4] For biographical note, see Appendix.

are able to see that no American is greater; that he was "the grandest figure on the crowded canvas of the nineteenth century"; that he represents the America we love as does no other man; that he abides and grows greater with the years; that there was in his simple figure an Olympian quality, a nobility and a grandeur; that he was of God; that it is fitting and proper his kneeling statue should be in this Cathedral; and that all of this greatness is revealed in the mood approaching religious awe which we feel when we visit his Memorial. One hundred and fifty years since his birth, and the outline of his figure, towering above his contemporaries, becomes clearer with the distance.

As preparation for this occasion I read with care his letters and addresses, trying to enter his mind and spirit that I might see his greatness from within and in some small manner understand it. The purpose of this address, and I hope of the whole sesquicentennial celebration, is that we may so understand him that something of his greatness will rub off onto our poorer natures.

There are, of course, some aspects of his figure which we will never understand, and at which we can only wonder. Trying to understand his strange combination of sorrow and jest, of loneliness and wit, is like gazing into a great forest; you can see so far, and then there is hidden mystery. Or how was it, to take another example, that in the midst of an age in which histrionic and florid oratory was the style, a man arose—with one year of formal schooling, poor, self-taught—who used language as a clean, chaste, and a simple expression of his thought? From what mysterious spring did he drink that he would not, could not, fit into the oratorical pattern of his day? And how was it that he who did not strive for beauty yet achieved it? We can never comprehend him, grasp him, wrap him up in a neat package; but we can from his writings see the broad outline of his greatness.

But, it is not enough to say that he was wise, moderate, merciful, forgiving, humane, a thinker of the first rank, and because of all these virtues the savior of the Union. We must try to go deeper than that, into the fabric of his mind and spirit, to see why he was these things. He looked at the world in a certain way; he reasoned in a certain manner; and then from the basic unity of his person the specific virtues arose. Great character is not a series of disconnected virtues—like a picket fence—but the great trunk of a tree that organically spreads out its strong branches.

Why was he so great? Why does the poet say that his deep spirit broods over this nation? Why, a few short years, after the most bitter of partisan struggles, was he accepted as a nonpartisan and unifying figure? Let me share with you my poor analysis, in which I have been helped by other men, and ask that you continue it in your own thoughts.

I

First, we live in a world where men tend to have their thoughts determined by their immediate interests and surroundings. They are white and think white, rich and think rich, easterners and think eastern. The tragedy of history is not simply that men are prone to obvious evil, but that they put their virtues and nobility at the service of their party or little group. Their virtues serve a limited perspective and a parochial imagination. How few Russians there are, for example, who are able to see the aspirations, interests, and fears of America—and vice versa! The result of this is enormous group egos that clash self-righteously with each other.

But occasionally, very occasionally, there appears a man like Lincoln, who mysteriously rises above background, self-interest, and even his age to think and speak for all men. He viewed the world in the deepest perspective, and had constantly about him the Olympian outlook. (See Richard Weaver, *The Ethics of Rhetoric.*) The Lincoln Memorial catches this; but you can see it also in his photographs with their homely grandeur and the far-away look in the eyes.

But most of all we can see this grand perspective in what Lord Charnwood calls the "arresting and simple beauty" of his language. "Four score and seven years ago our fathers"—the far-away look back across the long years to the founding of the nation. He deals with the Founding Fathers systematically and at length in the Cooper Union address that, knowing where they came from, his listeners may know where they are. Some men were violently from Massachusetts or South Carolina, but Lincoln had to say "brought forth on this *continent*" with a great sweep of thought. And then in the same address there is the far-away look into the future, "The world will little note, nor long remember, what we say here." Or again with the great perspective, "I shall do nothing in malice. What I deal with is too vast for malicious dealing." Or again, with the Olympian outlook above section or partisanship, "In the present Civil War it is quite possible that God's purpose is something different from the purpose of either party." Or again, the great inclusive view, "As I have not felt, so I have not expressed any harsh sentiment towards our southern brethren. I have constantly declared, as I really believed, the only difference between them and us, is the difference of circumstances." Or again, going beyond America, he states the meaning of America for all history and time—"that sentiment in the Declaration of Independence which gave liberty not alone to the people of this Country, but hope to all the world, for all future time."

It was from this perspective that the other virtues came. This is the trunk, and the other virtues are the branches; for if you have a true and great perspective, you know that you are only one actor in a vast drama—and humility is born. And, knowing the greatness of the cause and feeling the travail of a whole continent, you are willing to bear suffering and apologize if only the great cause may go forward. On October 24, 1862 he wrote to General McClellan with very human irritation, "I have just read your dispatch about sore-tongued and fatigued horses. Will you pardon me for asking what the horses of your army have done since the battle of Antietam that fatigues anything?" That is a temper like yours and mine. But three days later the great perspective rises again, "Yours of yesterday received," he writes to McClellan. "Most certainly I intend no injustice to any, and if I have done any, I deeply regret it."

II

Second, there was something truly remarkable about his method of reasoning. We all know that this self-educated man went deeper than most men, and that after a century much of what he said is still strangely fresh. Why is it, as Richard Weaver says, that he is more quoted than the more intellectual Jefferson or the academic Wilson? What can we learn about his method of reasoning?

Well, he was not corrupted by the modern advertising assumption that the average mental age is twelve years, or by a trust in promotional tricks that make all things trivial. He respected the people, and, as Herndon said, would not think of cheating a man out of his vote any more than he would cheat him out of his money. For his own sake and for his hearers he liked to boil a matter down to a terse statement. "I could not sleep, although I tried to, when I got on such a hunt for an idea until I had caught it; and when I thought I had got it, I was not satisfied until I had repeated it over and over again until I had put it in plain language enough, as I thought, for any boy I knew to comprehend. . . . This was a kind of passion with me." Herndon says that his opponents were afraid of his condensation. This means that Lincoln never threw a battery of arguments at people, like a scattering shotgun. He went to the essence of the matter; or, as he said, he liked to come at a question like a surveyor, from the north, south, east, and west until he had focused it. And then this essence was passed on to the people. "We won't break up the Union, and you shan't"; ". . . of the people, by the people, and for the people"; ". . . to do the right as God gives us to see the right." "Slavery is a violation of eternal right. We have temporized with it from the necessities of our condition; but as sure as God reigns and school children read, that black foul lie can never be consecrated into God's hallowed truth." These essences of a clear mind soaked down into the public consciousness until he was able to carry the people with him. He was, says Lord Charnwood, "free from ambiguity of thought or faltering of will."

But Herndon says another thing that brings us still closer to the secret of his power, and reveals the effect of his speaking. "All opponents dreaded his originality of idea, his condensation, definition, and force of expression; and woe to the man who hugged to his bosom a secret error if Lincoln got on the chase of it." Or again, "He was the strongest man I ever saw, looking at him from the standpoint of reason and logic. He came down from that height with irresistible and crashing force." Why? Well, partly the condensation we have already mentioned, but more profoundly the fact that he based his arguments on a definition of the nature of man, the nature of government, the nature of a nation, the nature of the war. This is why we quote him.

If you argue from expediency, your words will disappear in the sand; for the circumstances, upon which your expediency is based, will change. You will be clever, but not necessarily wise. But if you argue from the nature of man, from definition, your words will remain; because human nature does not change. Definition implies a general view which goes beyond the immediate circumstances. Definition requires courage, for you have committed yourself. Definition, based upon the nature of man, is reverent reasoning; for you are asserting the given fact, the final fact, the grain of the universe. So, slavery is attacked at dead center as contrary to the grain of the universe, corrupting the nature of the slave and the slaveholder. The facts of human nature, he believed, could be observed. It is God's decree which can never be reversed.

Is free government strong enough to survive, or must it always be smashed by a minority?—that was the basic question about the nature of free government which was being tested by the war. Or how, with the Father of Waters flowing through the middle of this nation, do you divide it north and south? The nature of a continent, the nature of man, the nature of government, the defined nature of the war. And, because he went in his reasoning to the one essential fact as distinguished from the peripheral and secondary, because he went to the argument behind which there is no other argument, his words endure. And some of them came out with thunder and finality. As Lord Charnwood said, he learned to reason with Euclid and to feel and speak with the authors of the Bible.

III

Finally, we consider the mystery of his religious stature which includes, of course, all we have said so far. This mystery is simply that of his total person. Formal education is good and necessary, but he was wise and profound without a formal education. Church membership with its means of grace and nurturing fellowship is good and necessary, but he was a saint in politics and a man of God without church membership. Just as in a lonely way he educated himself, so in a lonely way by reading the Scriptures and by profound meditation he nurtured his soul. "By their fruits shall ye know them"; and his good fruits reveal he was a good tree. If any man, freed from self, seeks the common good, he is a converted man, said William Temple—by that test he was a converted man. As a young man he was a skeptic, but the trials of his life drove him to God. He became a prophet bearing God's righteous and reconciling word to his people. While the church is as necessary for mankind as is the school, we must always recognize that "the wind bloweth where it listeth," and not try to domesticate the Almighty. We must, at the same time, recognize that in church attendance and Bible reading he did receive the Water of Life.

I first sensed his tremendous religious stature when his life helped to open up for me the meaning of the Beatitudes, which Senator Cooper read in the Second Lesson this afternoon. "Blessed are the merciful": kindness and mercy were in the fabric of his being. "Blessed are they who do hunger and thirst after righteousness"—"Beyond and above all skill," says the editor of a great newspaper who heard him at Peoria, "was the overwhelming conviction imposed upon the audience that the speaker was charged with an irresistible and inspiring duty to his fellow men."

"Blessed are the pure in heart": purity of heart is, apart from selfishness, to will one thing, that God's will be done and the good of all the people be served. "Blessed are the peacemakers." "Blessed are ye when men shall revile and persecute you, and say all manner of evil against you falsely for my sake." "Blessed are the poor in spirit," for, knowing their own need, and not arrogant in spirit, they turn to God in their need.

"Blessed are they that mourn"; if you truly love men, you must mourn when they die in battle. Sorrow is the other side of the coin of love.

"Blessed are the meek": meekness is the opposite of self-centered pushiness. It is to be so centered in God's great purposes that one's own little ego is out of the picture. Lincoln refused to be angry when McClellan snubbed him, even insulted him. He wrote to General Grant:

> When you got below and took Port Gibson, Grand Gulf, and vicinity, I thought you should go down the river and join General Banks, and when you turned northward, east of the Big Black, I feared it was a mistake. I now wish to make the personal acknowledgment that you were right and I was wrong. Sincerely, Abraham Lincoln.

"Blessed are the meek."

Before closing with three passages in which we will listen to Lincoln's own words, consider this description of how it appeared to those who heard him. "As soon as he lost thought of himself in his subject his voice and manner changed; deeper notes, of which friends record the beauty, rang out, the sad eyes kindled, and the tall, gaunt figure with the strange gesture of the long, uplifted arms, acquired even a certain majesty."

(a) He said about a Negro slave:

> In some things she is certainly not my equal, but in her natural right to eat the bread that she has earned with the sweat of her brow, she is my equal, and the equal of Judge Douglas, and the equal of any man.

(b) He said:

> I know there is a God, and that he hates injustice and slavery. I see the storm coming, and I know that His hand is in it. If He has a place and work for me—and I think He has—I believe I am ready. I am nothing, but truth is everything. I know I am right because I know that liberty is right, for Christ teaches it, and Christ is God. I have told them that a house divided against itself cannot stand, and Christ and reason say the same; and they will find it so. Douglas don't care whether slavery is voted up or voted down, but God cares, and humanity cares, and I care; and with God's help I shall not fail. I may not see the end; but it will come, and I shall be vindicated; and these men will find that they have not read their Bible aright.

(c) He said:

When . . . you have succeeded in dehumanizing the Negro; when you have put him down and made it impossible for him to be but as the beasts of the field; when you have extinguished his soul in this world and placed him where the ray of hope is blown out as in the darkness of the damned, are you quite sure that the demon you have roused will not turn and rend you? What constitutes the bulwark of our own liberty and independence? It is not our frowning battlements, our bristling sea coasts, our army and navy. These are not our reliance against tyranny. All of those may be turned against us without making us weaker for the struggle. Our reliance is in the love of liberty which God has planted in us. Our defense is in the spirit which prized liberty as the heritage of all men, in all lands everywhere. Destroy this spirit and you have planted the seeds of despotism at your own doors. Familiarize yourselves with the chains of bondage and you prepare your own limbs to wear them. Accustomed to trample on the rights of others, you have lost the genius of your own independence and become the fit subject of the first cunning tyrant who rises among you.

Praise be to thee, O God, for thy servant and prophet, Abraham Lincoln.

APPENDIX

BIOGRAPHICAL NOTES

ASHMORE, HARRY SCOTT (1916-). Born, Greenville, South Carolina; B.S., Clemson Agricultural College, 1937; LL.D., Oberlin College, 1958; reporter, Greenville *Piedmont,* 1937-39; political writer Greenville *News,* 1939-41; Nieman Fellow, Harvard University, 1941; served with United States Army in 95th Infantry Division, advancing from lieutenant to lieutenant colonel, 1942-45; in Rhineland, northern France, and central European campaigns, with Operations Division of War Department General Staff, 1945; cited for special duty, receiving Bronze Star and other awards; associate editor, Charlotte *News,* 1945-47; editor, later executive editor, *Arkansas Gazette,* Little Rock, 1947- ; directed forty scholars under Ford Foundation Fund for the Advancement of Education program to study biracial education in the United States, 1953; upheld 1954 Supreme Court desegration decision and in 1957 criticized stand of Governor Orval Faubus; awarded the $1,000 Pulitzer Prize for editorial writing, May 1958; author, *The Negro and the Schools,* 1954; *An Epitaph for Dixie,* 1958. (See also *Current Biography, 1958).*

BLAKELY, ROBERT J. (1915-). Born, Nebraska; A.B., State University of Iowa, 1937; graduate study in history, Harvard University, 1937-38; editorial writer, Des Moines *Register and Tribune,* 1938-42; Office of War Information, special assistant to Gardner Cowles, Jr., director of domestic branch, 1942-43; United States Marine Corps Reserves, 1943-45, commissioned, 1944; forward observer for artillery with the 3rd and 6th Marine Divisions; wounded, Okinawa, discharged as first lieutenant; with *Register and Tribune,* 1946-48; editorial writer, St. Louis *Star-Times,* 1948-51; manager of the central regional office of the Ford Foundation Fund for Adult Education, 1951-56; vice president of the Fund, 1956-   ; author of articles in *Foreign Affairs* and other periodicals, Council on Foreign Relations publications; *Adult Education in a Free Society* (collection of his speeches).

BLOUGH, ROGER M. (1904-   ). Born, Riverside, Pennsylvania; A.B., Susquehanna University, 1925, LL.D., 1953; LL.B., Yale University, 1931; LL.D., Baylor University, 1955, Washington and Jefferson College, 1956; admitted to bar, practicing in New York and Pennsylvania courts and before United States Supreme Court; practiced law with White and Case, New York City, 1931-42; general solicitor, United States Steel Corporation of Delaware, 1942-51; named executive vice president (law) and secretary, U.S. Steel, 1951; chairman of board of directors and chief executive officer, 1955-   . (See also *Current Biography: 1955.)*

DULLES, JOHN FOSTER (1888-1959). Born, Washington, D.C.; B.A., Princeton University, 1908, LL.D., 1946; Sorbonne, Paris, 1908-09; LL.B., George Washington University, 1911; LL.D., Tufts College, Wagner College, Northwestern University; law practice, New York City, 1911-49; director, Bank of New York; trustee, Rockefeller Foundation; chairman, Carnegie Endowment for International Peace; chairman, Federal Council of Churches Commission on a Just and Durable Peace; secretary to a delegation, Hague Peace Conference, 1907; captain and major, United States Army, 1917-18; member, Reparations Commission and Supreme Economic Council, 1919; member, United States delegation, San Francisco Conference on World Organization, 1945; Council of Foreign Ministers, London, 1945; General Assembly, United Nations, 1946; adviser, meeting of Council of Foreign Ministers, Moscow, and London meeting of "Big Four," 1947; United States Senate (Republican, New York), July-November 1949 (appointed to complete term of Senator Wagner); appointed counselor, Department of State, April 1950; appointed, with rank of ambassador, to negotiate terms of peace for Japan, 1951; representative at signing of Japanese peace treaty, San Francisco, 1951; writer and speaker on international affairs; author, *War or Peace,* 1950; appointed Secretary of State in the Eisenhower cabinet, 1953; resigned as Secretary of State, appointed special adviser, April 1959; died, May 24, 1959. (See also *Current Biography: 1953.*)

EISENHOWER, DWIGHT D. (1890-). Born, Denison, Texas; B.S., United States Military Academy, 1915; Army Tank School, 1921; graduate, War College, 1929; second lieutenant, United States Army, 1915; lieutenant colonel, Tank Corps, World War I; advanced through grades to General of the Army, December 1944; Chief of Operations Division, Office of Chief of Staff, 1942; Allied Commander in Chief, North Africa, November 1942; Supreme Commander of Allied Land, Sea, and Air Forces in Western Europe, November 1943; Chief of Staff, United States Army, 1945-48; president, Columbia University, 1948-52; appointed Supreme Commander of the North Atlantic Treaty Organization, 1950; elected President of the United States, November 1952; suffered coronary thrombosis, September 1955; reelected President, November 1956; underwent operation for ileitis, June 1956; suffered mild stroke, November 1957; author, *Crusade in Europe,* 1948; *Eisenhower Speaks,* 1948. (See also *Current Biography: 1957.)*

EMRICH, RICHARD STANLEY MERRILL (1910-). Born, Mardin, Turkey (parents United States citizens); A.B., Brown University, 1932, LL.D., 1949; student, Episcopal Theological School, 1932-33; B.D., Union Theological Seminary, 1935; Ph.D., University of Marburg, 1937; S.T.D., Kenyon College, 1948; D.D., Huron College, Ontario, 1950; LL.D., Rensselaer, 1955; ordained minister, Episcopal Church, 1936; instructor, assistant professor, and professor, Episcopal Theological School, Cambridge, Massachusetts, 1937-46; rector, South Lincoln, Massachusetts, 1937-40; Marion, Massachusetts, 1944-46; suffragan bishop of Michigan, 1946-48; bishop of Michigan, 1948- ; member, Phi Beta Kappa; author, *The Conception of the Church in the Writings of Baron von Hügel,* 1938; *Earth Might Be Fair,* 1945.

FULBRIGHT, JAMES WILLIAM (1905-). Born, Sumner, Missouri; A.B., University of Arkansas, 1925; B.A., Oxford University (Rhodes scholar), 1928, M.A., 1931; LL.B., George Washington University, 1934; admitted to District of Columbia bar, 1934; special attorney, antitrust division, United States Department of Justice, 1934-35; instructor in law, George Washington University, 1935-36, University of Arkansas, 1936-39; president, University of Arkansas, 1939-41; United States House of Representatives (Democrat, Arkansas), 1943-45; Senate, 1945- ; author of the Fulbright act setting up grants for foreign study and research, 1946. (See also *Current Biography: 1955.)*

HOOVER, HERBERT CLARK (1874-). Born, West Branch, Iowa; B.A. in engineering, Stanford University, 1895; honorary degrees from Brown University, Columbia University, Johns Hopkins University, Oxford University, University of Prague, and other institutions here and abroad; United States Food Administrator, 1917-19; director of various relief organizations for the war-stricken nations of Europe; appointed Secretary of Commerce in 1921; Republican President of the United States, 1929-1933; coordinator of food supplies to thirty-eight countries, 1946; chairman, Committee on Organization of the Executive Branch of the Government, 1947-49; member, advisory board, International Bank for Reconstruction and Development; chairman, Committee on Government Operations, July 1953; author, *American Individualism,* 1922; *The Challenge to Liberty,* 1934; *Addresses Upon the American Road,* 1933-55; *The Ordeal of Woodrow Wilson,* 1958. (See also *Current Biography: 1943.)*

HUMPHREY, HUBERT HORATIO, JR. (1911-). Born, Wallace, South Dakota; student, Denver School of Pharmacy, 1932-33; A.B., University of Minnesota, 1939; A.M., University of Louisiana, 1940; graduate studies, University of Minnesota, 1940-41; LL.B., law school, National University, Washington; assistant instructor, political science, University of Louisiana, 1939-40, Univerity of Minnesota, 1940-41; member of administrative staff, Works Progress Administration; assistant state supervisor, later director of adult education in Minnesota; state director of war production training and reemployment, later chief of state war service program, 1941-43; assistant regional director, War Manpower Commission, 1943; professor of political science, Macalester College, 1943-44; mayor of Minneapolis, 1945-48; United States Senate (Democrat, Minnesota), 1949- ; visited the U.S.S.R. and interviewed Premier Khrushchev, 1958; member, Phi Beta Kappa, Delta Sigma Rho. (See also *Current Biography: 1949.*)

KENNEDY, JOHN FITZGERALD (1917-). Born, Brookline, Massachusetts; student, London School of Economics, 1935-36; B.S., *cum laude,* Harvard University, 1940; LL.D., University of Notre Dame, 1950, Tufts College, 1954, Harvard University, 1956; served in United States Navy, 1941-45, awarded Purple Heart and other military decorations; correspondent, San Francisco United Nations Conference, British election, Potsdam Meeting, 1945; United States House of Representatives (Democrat, Massachusetts), 1947-53; Senate, 1953- ; author, *Why England Slept,* 1940; *Profiles in Courage,* 1956 (Pulitzer Prize for biography). (See also *Current Biography: 1950.)*

MCDONALD, DAVID JOHN (1902-). Born, Pittsburgh, Pennsylvania; student, Duquesne University, 1921; graduate, drama school of Carnegie Institute of Technology, 1932; steelworker, secretary and assistant to vice president, United Mine Workers of America, 1923-36; secretary-treasurer, Steel Workers Organization Committee, 1936-42; international secretary, United Steelworkers of America (CIO), 1942-53, president, 1953- , vice president, AFL-CIO; secretary-treasurer, Political Action Committee; director, American Arbitration Association; author, *Coal and Unionism,* 1939. (See also *Current Biography: 1953.)*

MEANY, GEORGE (1894-). Born, New York City; attended elementary and high schools, New York City; journeyman plumber, 1915; business representative, Plumbers' Local Union, 1922-34; president, New York State Federation of Labor, 1934-39; secretary-treasurer, American Federation of Labor, 1940-52, president, 1952-55; president, AFL-CIO, December 1955- . (See also *Current Biography: 1954.)*

NIXON, RICHARD MILHOUS (1913-). Born, Yorba Linda, California; A.B., Whittier College, 1934; LL.B., Duke University Law School, 1937; general practice of law, Whittier, California, 1937-43; attorney with Office of Emergency Management, Washington, D.C., 1942; lieutenant-commander, United States Navy, 1942-46; member, House of Representatives (Republican, California), 1947-50; Senate, 1951-52; elected Vice President of the United States on the Republican ticket, 1952 and 1956. (See also *Current Biography: 1958.)*

ROCKEFELLER, NELSON ALDRICH (1908-). Born, Bar Harbor, Maine; A.B., Dartmouth College, 1930; director, Rockefeller Center, Inc., 1931- , president, 1938-45, 1948-51; chairman, 1945-53, 1956-58; coordinator of Inter-American Affairs, 1940-44; assistant secretary of state, 1944-45; chairman, international development advisory board, Point Four Program, 1950-51; undersecretary of Health, Education and Welfare, 1953-54; special assistant to President, 1954-55; elected Republican governor of New York, 1958; officer, Museum of Modern Art, Rockefeller Brothers Fund, Inc., American International Association for Economic and Social Development, International Basic Economy Corporation; awarded orders of merit by Chile, Brazil, Mexico; member Phi Beta Kappa. (See also *Current Biography: 1951.)*

SEVAREID, ERIC (1912-). Born, Velva, North Dakota, A.B., University of Minnesota, 1935; student, Alliance Française, Paris, 1937; reporter, Minneapolis *Journal,* 1931, Minneapolis *Star,* 1936-37; reporter, city editor, Paris edition of New York *Herald Tribune,* 1938-39; European correspondent, Columbia Broadcasting System, 1939; with French Army and Air Force in France and Belgium during World War II; broadcast from England, Holland, Belgium, Luxembourg, Mexico, Brazil; now CBS correspondent; past president, Radio Correspondents Association; author, *Not So Wild a Dream,* 1946; *In One Ear,* 1952; *Small Sounds in the Night,* 1956. (See also *Current Biography: 1942.)*

SIZOO, JOSEPH RICHARD (1885-). Born in The Netherlands; brought to the United States, 1891; A.B., Hope College, 1907, A.M., 1910, D.D., 1925; B.D., New Brunswick Theological Seminary, 1910; graduate work, Columbia University; D.D., Rutgers University, 1930; Litt.D., Hastings College, 1932; S.T.D., Columbia University, 1938; LL.D., George Washington University, 1934; ordained in ministry of Reformed Church in America, 1910; missionary in southern India, 1910-11; minister, Walden, New York, 1911-17; Somerville, New Jersey, 1917-24; pastor, New York Avenue Presbyterian Church, Washington, D.C., 1924-36; St. Nicholas Collegiate Church, New York City, 1936-47; president, New Brunswick Theological Seminary, 1947-52; professor of religion, George Washington University, 1952- ; army chaplain, YMCA service, overseas, World War I; chaplain, 12th Regiment, New York National Guard; awarded Huguenot Annual Award, 1954; author, *Abraham Lincoln, William Jennings Bryan, The Kingdom Cometh, Our Faiths, The Way of Faith, Make Life Worth Living, On Guard, Preaching Unashamed.*

THONSSEN, LESTER (1904-). Born, Sutherland, Iowa; A.B., Huron College, 1926; A.M., State University of Iowa, 1929; Ph.D., 1931; D.Lit., Huron College, 1958; instructor of speech, Pacific University, 1926-28; instructor of speech, later assistant professor, associate professor, professor, City College of New York, 1931- ; visiting professor, summer sessions, Montana State University, State University of Iowa, University of Colorado, University of Southern California, University of Hawaii, Teachers College, Columbia University; editor, *Speech Monographs,* 1948-50; president, Speech Association of America, 1956; author or co-author, *Bibliography of Speech Education, Speech Criticism, Basic Training in Speech,* and other books.

TRUMAN, HARRY S. (1884-). Born, Lamar, Missouri; student, Kansas City School of Law, 1923-25; captain, Field Artillery, World War I; judge, Jackson County Court, 1922-24; presiding judge, 1926-34; United States Senate (Democrat, Missouri), 1935-45; elected Vice President of the United States on the Democratic ticket, November 1944; sworn in as President on the death of President Roosevelt, April 1945; elected President, 1948; refused candidacy for reelection and retired, January 1953; author, *Memoirs (Year of Decisions, Years of Trial and Hope)*, 1955-56. (See also *Current Biography: 1945*.)

CUMULATIVE AUTHOR INDEX

An author index to the volumes of *Representative American Speeches* for the years 1937-1938 through 1958-1959. The date preceding the title of each speech indicates the volume in which it appears.